'In this book Judy Ryde makes an impassioned and well-argued contribution to the ever-growing body of work on whiteness which is designed to challenge what people who are read as racially white think about themselves. Building on her earlier contribution rooted in her work in caring professions and particularly psychotherapy, this new work takes a broader stance to consider the social damage wreaked by socially constructed racial hierarchy where whiteness is positioned at the pinnacle.

Anyone interested in making reparation for the privileges and wages of whiteness should read this book!'

– Dr Shona Hunter, reader in Race Education and Decoloniality at Leeds Beckett University, and author of Power Politics and the Emotions: Impossible Governance

'A long awaited and comprehensive resource for all interested in how white people are still benefiting by their privilege and the role that white supremacy plays in our understanding of this. It is an unusual book as Judy is herself white. Essential reading if you identify as white and if you don't!'

– Rotimi Akinsete, therapeutic counsellor, clinical supervisor, Director of Wellbeing at the University of Surrey and founder and director of Black Men on the Couch, focussing on psychotherapy and identity politics of African and Caribbean men and boys

'Written in an accessible and engaging style, this book not only charts where white privilege comes from, but also offers possible ways we can start to challenge society's structural inequalities. In doing so, it boldly examines one of the most divisive, yet important and powerful, social constructs of our time: race.'

– Sarah Hackett, Reader in Modern European History, Bath Spa University and author of Foreigners, Minorities and Integration: The Muslim Immigrant Experience in Britain and Germany

by the same author

Being White in the Helping Professions
Developing Effective Intercultural Awareness
Judy Ryde
ISBN 978 1 84985 667 6
eISBN 978 1 84642 730 5

of related interest

Using Art Techniques Across Cultural and Race Boundaries
Working with Identity
Lorette Dye
ISBN 978 1 78592 234 3
eISBN 978 1 78450 512 7

Autism and Ethnicity
Working with Children and Families with Autism
from Minority Ethnic Communities
Prithvi Perepa
ISBN 978 1 78592 360 9
eISBN 978 1 78450 701 5

Dementia, Culture and Ethnicity
Issues for All
Edited by Julia Botsford and Karen Harrison Dening
Foreword by Alistair Burns
ISBN 978 1 84905 486 7
eISBN 978 0 85700 881 7

Working with Ethnicity, Race and Culture in Mental Health
A Handbook for Practitioners
Hári Sewell
ISBN 978 1 84310 621 0
eISBN 978 1 84642 855 5

WHITE PRIVILEGE

UNMASKED

....

How to Be Part of the Solution

....

Judy Ryde

Jessica Kingsley *Publishers*
London and Philadelphia

First published in 2019
by Jessica Kingsley Publishers
73 Collier Street
London N1 9BE, UK
and
400 Market Street, Suite 400
Philadelphia, PA 19106, USA

www.jkp.com

Library of Congress Cataloging in Publication Data
A CIP catalog record for this book is available from the Library of Congress

British Library Cataloguing in Publication Data
A CIP catalogue record for this book is available from the British Library

ISBN 978 1 78592 408 8
eISBN 978 1 78450 767 1

Printed and bound in Great Britain

Contents

Acknowledgements

Many people have helped and supported me in writing this book. My biggest support has been my husband, Peter Hawkins, who read and commented on all drafts. He has always been there to encourage me and to discuss my ideas – and come up with suggestions. It would have been hard to have written it without his support.

Michaela Von Britzka has also provided very strong support by reading through drafts and making useful comments with wonderful enthusiasm and perspicacity.

I would also like to acknowledge: my sister, Cath Ryde, who read through chapters and gave useful feedback; Peter Reason for being interested and encouraging and sending many useful suggestions for reading; Alan Rosen for many exchanges about reparation, including information about his work with First Nation Australians.

The following have been supportive and offered useful perspectives: Addy Adelaine, Catherine Carr, June Hall, Kristina Lindstrand, Liz Mason and Barbara Walsh.

PART 1

....

FACING UP TO WHITE PRIVILEGE

....

CHAPTER 1

Introduction

We live in a world that is imbued with the idea that the human population is divided into races (Irvin Painter, 2010:119; Kendi, 2016:18). This may not always be obvious, particularly if we are white and live mostly among white people. White people do not usually think of themselves as 'having' a race, but in this book, I will challenge the attitude, often held by white people, that they are racially and culturally neutral (Dyer, 1997; Frankenberg, 1999; Kincheloe & Steinberg, 1998). We live within a racialised world, in other words, one in which all are divided into different races (Bonnett, 2000). Although originally thought to have a biological basis (Mahoney, 1997), this has been thoroughly discredited. Nevertheless, race is still very much a powerful social construct that influences the way we relate to others.

This book has many challenges to white people. I challenge the idea that white people are without a race, that our political arrangements are superior to others, that we have liberal-minded and fair societies, that past injustices are in the past and that we, on the whole, have been a net positive for the world, particularly as our technologies have actually brought the world to the possibility of extinction. This hard-hitting quote from Susan Sontag, written as long ago as 1967, puts this very well:

> The truth is that Mozart, Pascal, Boolean and Algebra, Shakespeare, Parliamentary Democracy, Baroque Churches, Newton, the emancipation of women, Kant, Marx, Balanchine ballets *et al.*, don't redeem what this particular civilization has wrought upon the world. The white races are the cancer of human history; it is the white race and it alone – its ideologies and inventions – which eradicates autonomous civilizations wherever it spreads, which has

upset the ecological balance of the planet, which now threatens the very existence of life itself. (Sontag, 1967:57)

This book is based on two connected ideas. The first is to show how white people are over-privileged compared with other races. The second is that white privilege will come to an end before too long. I hope this book will demonstrate how white people can, nevertheless, contribute positively to the way in which power is distributed worldwide in the future by not denying or clinging on to their privilege.

Reaching these thoughts has been a long journey. When I was a child I was surrounded by white people and I only had a few images of black people to inform my knowledge of them. One was from a children's geography book that depicted Africans dancing round a fire holding spears. I also remember well the story of Little Black Sambo, which was not considered racist at the time. It just depicted a little boy who saved his family from a tiger. These depictions nevertheless gave the impression of rather simple people, particularly through the illustrations, and no doubt had an effect on my sense of who black people were. My gollywog was one of my favorite toys and I remember having a feeling of loss when, in my late teens, I came to realise that this stylised black soft toy with big features and fuzzy hair, who was incongruously dressed in a red jacket, striped trousers and bow tie, should be rejected as a racist artefact. I even saved tokens from jars of jam to acquire a 'golly' brooch. A warm memory of my childhood was destroyed. Although there is a way in which I was an innocent child delighting in a toy without any knowledge of its meaning in the wider world, it nevertheless affected my sense of who black people are, as it does all people who are given such representations of black people as children.

It did not occur to my parents, who were liberal-minded socialists, that there was anything wrong with these influences and images. They taught me that it was wrong to be prejudiced against black people but my mother, for instance, if referring to a black man, would say that he was a 'coloured gentleman' in a slightly coy voice. The impression was that she thought she was being broad minded in calling him a gentleman. These sorts of influences go very deep and have no doubt affected me to this very day, although I now see myself as being white within a multicultural society. At some other level, these formative experiences cannot be eradicated.

My first real encounter with a black person was a Nigerian friend at school who became my 'best friend' when I was about 14. When I was 12 we heard that a Nigerian girl was coming to the school and there was some discussion about what colour her skin would be. One girl said she would be black all over and I said that the palms of her hands would be white, which was strenuously denied by the others. When we saw her palms, no one was quite sure what colour they were, so it wasn't mentioned. She was often mocked by some of the children at school – called Coco, for example. There was no attempt to curb this behaviour by the teachers. The drama teacher made her 'white up' with pink make-up to be in the Chorus in Shakespeare's *Henry V*, in spite of the fact she could well have played this role as a black person without it being very radical. It made her look ridiculous, but she bore it with fortitude. When we left school at the age of 18, she came to understand the racism she had encountered and she rejected us all. It was a great sadness to me at the time, and remains so. I have often tried to find her through the internet when such things became possible – so far unsuccessfully.

I did not seriously think of myself as being white until I started my doctoral research in the late 1990s although, if asked, I would have said I was white. I discovered that, like me, most white people do not think of themselves as having a race at all. I was nevertheless interested in cultural difference and promoting racial equality and understanding. Maybe my experience with my school friend led me to be concerned with these issues most of my life. However, I thought of this concern as coming from a desire to challenge racist views and work for equality and understanding between races.

It was through my doctoral research that I came to see that the problem of racism starts with white people and that, if I am to understand racism, I must first understand myself and the culture in which I am embedded as a white person. This journey continues and, having started with my doctoral research and subsequently written a book about being white – *Being White in the Helping Professions* (Ryde, 2009) – I know there is always more to explore, learn and understand.

It is important for me to remember, as I write this book, that it is impossible for me not to write from inside my own experience. This is also true of the reader when reading it – you can only read it in the light of your own experience. I am white. I come from a culture that is implacably imbued with white experience and a sense of entitlement. I look out of those eyes and see the world from that perspective, however hard I try not to do so.

Of course, like other human beings, I can be self-reflective and empathetic to others. I can have good intentions and desire to change. But I can never really and thoroughly experience the world from an other-than-white perspective. This, of course, limits me but does put me in a good position to challenge other white people, including, but not only, those in the helping professions such as social workers, counsellors and psychotherapists, and that is the purpose of writing this book. It is an important challenge, as finding a way to create and work towards a more equal world is vital. The destructive power of global inequality (Wilkinson & Pickett, 2009) leads some people and nations to live in poverty, while others are vastly more wealthy. Besides the conflict this inevitably brings, it also leads to the rich (mostly white) nations over-exploiting the world's resources, which is the biggest threat to the flourishing of life on earth, and even its survival. Towards the end of this book, in Chapter 13, I will be exploring how a more equal global society can lead to a more peaceful and sustainable world.

Since writing the book *Being White in the Helping Professions* (Ryde, 2009), I have defined white people as those who are from western Europe or the diaspora that originated there. It therefore includes many people now living in North America, South Africa, Australia, New Zealand and other countries where western Europeans settled and colonised.

Originally it was assumed, by explorers and travellers and later by scientists, that there was a hierarchy of human races, Anglo Saxons being at the top and 'Negros' at the bottom (Irvin Painter, 2010; Kendi, 2016). Although it is now well known that 'race' as a category has no physiological basis (Cambell & Oakes, 1998; Mahoney, 1997), attitudes that arise from this idea persist and appear to be engrained in the human psyche, as we will see as this book unfolds. I will explore the history of 'white' as a racial category in Chapter 2.

Much of what I have described above has not changed since I wrote my book in 2009 but, although less than a decade has passed between then and writing this book, the world has moved on in various significant ways that make a difference to the position of white people globally. This will be explored in later chapters but suffice it to say at this point, changes in the economic power of Asian nations are set to transform the balance of power globally, and the further spread of wars in the Middle East and the rise of nationalism and far-right politics in Europe and America have brought with them a global 'perfect storm' which could force change more quickly than seemed likely to me a few years ago.

So why do I use the word 'privilege' in the title of this book? It was western Europeans who named themselves as white and saw others as 'people of colour', whether brown, black, red or yellow. Other writers used other, quasi-scientific names such as Caucasian, Mongoloid and Negroid (Alcoff, 2015; Baum, 2008; Irvin Painter, 2010). They imagined themselves, as white people, to be more capable and intelligent than those from other races. They saw non-whites as being available for their own use, much as they liked to think of animals (Irvin Painter, 2010). The history of this will be briefly outlined in the next chapter. It is not an exhaustive history of all white peoples. For instance, I do not give much mention to the European colonisation of South America. I hope, nevertheless, that I have written enough to show how deep the underpinning of white peoples' sense of superiority goes, and the way their historical determination to enforce dominance has given them an ability to sit in a privileged position, with benefits that continue to this day.

It comes home to me more and more that white people tend to see racial prejudice as a problem black people have, but it would not even exist as a problem if white people had not invented it and put themselves on the top of the pile. In her book, *Notes on a Foreign Country*, Suzy Hansen (2017: 89) says:

> The revelation to me was not that black people had conceived of their identities in response to ours, but that our white identities had been composed in conscious objection to *theirs*. I'd had no idea that we had ever had to define our identities at all, because to me, white Americans were born fully formed, completely detached from any sort of complicated past. Even now, I can remember that shiver of recognition that only comes when you learn something that expands, just a tiny bit, your sense of reality.

This book is an exploration of white privilege within the context of a world in which the idea of 'race' affects the relationship between groups of people in a way that provokes dangerous conflict, unthinking prejudice and disastrous misunderstanding. As recently as the second half of the 20th century, with laws prohibiting racial prejudice in many countries globally, it seemed to me, and those I knew at the time, that the world was heading for greater racial equality. In recent years, there has been a marked upsurge in the rise of far-right nationalistic political parties and politicians in Europe such as Alternative für Deutschland (Alternative for Germany), Front National in France, Freiheitliche Partei Österreichs (Freedom Party of Austria), The Finns in Finland, The Danish People's Party, Partij voor de Vrijheid (Party for Freedom) in Holland, Lega Nord (North League) in Italy, Sverigedemokraterna (Sweden Democrats) and The UK Independence Party in Britain. They all have nationalistic sentiments, want to greatly restrict immigration and are enthusiastically followed by a great percentage of the population of each country, if not the majority. They can no longer be considered to be on the very fringes of the electorate. To a party, they have welcomed Donald Trump who has, of course, been the most successful far-right politician and came to power almost in spite of the American Republican Party. With the UK voting to leave the European Union (Brexit) and Donald Trump becoming President of the USA, it now seems that progress towards racial equality has halted or even reversed.

Today's world is rapidly changing. It is becoming more and more interlinked as globalisation becomes the norm (Menzies, 2016) and digital technology advances exponentially, but it is also under great pressure from over population and crises due to climate change and political, often violent, upheavals. These changes are complex and frequently connected with each other (Fioramonti, 2016). This will be explored in more detail in Chapters 4 and 13.

This book is written with the 'helping' professions in mind (doctors, nurses, social workers, psychologists, psychotherapists and counsellors) but will be of interest much more widely, including to anyone who is interested in thinking about what will help us to live in a more just, peaceful and equal world. We all live and work within a racialised society and it behoves us to understand the complex way in which cultural attitudes affect individuals and groups within it.

Even workplaces and professions have their own culture which ensures that they are blind to their own prejudices. My own profession of psycho-therapy, for instance, is very slow to be more diverse in spite of an espoused desire to become less monocultural. The vast majority of its practitioners are white. This, in itself, has a huge effect on the experience of non-white people, many of whom think that psychotherapy is not for them.

That is not to say that psychotherapy as a profession has nothing to offer those who are not white (Ryde, 2009). Some of the insights that originate in psychotherapy theorising can be useful to understand these issues and I will draw on them in this book. I will also draw on the work of sociologists, anthropologists, social workers, economists, historians, philosophers and human rights activists who write about 'whiteness' within a racialised context. There is not an extensive literature about whiteness compared with other aspects of race and culture and almost all that exists has been written by non-white people, which is further evidence that it is hard for white people to understand that there is an issue of importance here.

As a psychotherapist, I have understood, through training and experience, that if we are to learn and change we need to first understand ourselves. Thus, when I came to undertake research in the area of intercultural psychotherapy, it was natural to me to start with myself. When it comes to race, my racial identity is white so that is where I start. Therefore, while this book may be of interest to those who identify as non-white, the main thrust is a challenge to white people to understand themselves as being white with all that entails and, in particular, the way in which racial inequality intertwines with culture and class (Hill Collins & Bilge, 2016; Kendi, 2016) and affects conflicts worldwide. I will explore intersectionality and identity politics in Chapter 7.

It seems that we are now seeing a reaction to white dominance and privilege from other nations, cultures and races as well as a backlash from white people who fear losing this status, particularly those who are themselves disadvantaged in other ways but can at least claim this privilege (Eddo-Lodge, 2017). The era which, not so long ago, allowed white people to feel good about themselves merely because they advocate equal rights for all people and declare themselves not to be racist seems to be coming to an end. White people can no longer leave their own culpability unchallenged and not acknowledge the way that they are responsible for inequalities that still exist and have their roots in our history, behaviour and actions.

So, my contention is that, in order to address issues caused by racial tensions, we must understand ourselves more fully and admit our culpability more honestly. To do that we need to begin by understanding the history of race as a concept. We need to grasp that it was introduced by white people as a way of portraying themselves as superior and others as inferior. This has allowed white people to abuse, dominate and exploit non-white people over the centuries, including by forcing people into slavery, colonising other lands and even ethnic cleansing, where whole nations of indigenous people have been systematically decimated or eliminated, for instance, in the USA and Australia (Irvin Painter, 2010). White, European countries became rich and powerful through this exploitation and we still benefit from this today (Kendi, 2016). Our being white is embedded in this history and our very natures and cultural concepts are imbued with this dynamic. Not being aware of this as part of the problem exacerbates the situation, and I will explore this in Chapter 3.

We can look at the larger picture and towards history to better understand where we are today, and we can also look to our own attitudes, assumptions and motivations for greater insights. We will therefore seek to understand whiteness holistically, in our history, cultural arrangements and attitudes as well as how this shows up in our subjective experience. We are embedded in the culture of our interconnecting societies. In this way, we can bring to mind a clear picture of racial and cultural dis-ease in today's world. Most importantly, this exploration and self-reflection will help lead us towards making significant changes in the world, starting with ourselves. We do not exist as separate, watertight entities but are deeply embedded in our culture and society just as our culture and society are embedded in us. Accordingly, a change in our own consciousness brings with it a wider change and will be a step towards bringing about a transformation towards greater justice and equality. Wilkinson and Pickett have shown that the more equal the world is the more it is peaceful and content (2009). I will draw on their work extensively.

The self-reflection I am advocating goes beyond cognitive understanding. It affects our hearts as well as our minds. I explore this by demonstrating the interconnected nature of our lives. I explain the methodologies of dialogue and inquiry which can help us to understand how we are systemically embedded within and between cultures. In my view, this is the key to genuine understanding and real change, rather than superficial and ineffective change. This is discussed in Chapter 8.

Whether or not we are able to live more peacefully as white people, we may be forced to adapt to changes in the world, as those outside the white, western world become more confident and wealthier. Because of white suppositions about the superiority of their own ways, it tends to be assumed that other countries, like China and India, who become wealthy will fall into line behind the USA and other western countries and become just richer members of the global, elite, western community. This may well not be the case. I explore this further in Chapters 5 and 13.

Because the terms 'race', 'black' and 'white' and other such words are constructed ideas which arise from prejudice rather than something biological, it is not always easy to decide which words to use. The term 'white' is quite slippery and who falls under its definition is not always clear. I therefore sometimes use the term 'non-white' as well as 'black'. I also use the word 'West' and 'western' to describe the parts of the world where white people tend to live. Within the term 'West', I mean to include Australia and New Zealand even though they are clearly not in the west of the globe. They are, though, part of the white world. Black and non-white people increasingly live in the 'West' and this allows me to have a word that covers this fact.

There are three parts to this book. The first is called 'Facing Up to White Privilege' and shows how we have reached the situation we are in today where 'white' has become the most privileged, but the least described, race globally.

The second part is called 'The Effects of White Privilege' and concerns the conflict and struggles that have resulted from this divisive way of designating populations worldwide and the political and personal attitudes and assumptions that have resulted.

Part 3, 'Making Personal and Societal Changes', explores how we might respond to racism and white privilege as white people and gives methodologies for taking forward and acting on the ideas discussed in this book, including making reparations rather than just deliberating on them.

The conclusion will bring the ideas of the book together and look to the needs of the future and how we might respond to the challenges that are coming over the horizon. In a fast-changing world, we need to be aware that we can never rest on our laurels, since the future is likely to bring fresh and complex challenges.

CHAPTER 2

A Short History of White as a Racial Category

To comprehend the depth to which white privilege is rooted in white society, it is important to understand the history behind it. Our historically inherited culture has a huge influence on our lives, and the economic advantage, which is part and parcel of our history, is a legacy that imbues the cultural setting into which we are born. It gives us certain attitudes and accepted ways of being and behaving, as well as the way that we experience the world (Gapp & Bohacek, 2017). We *are* our history. It is not only a matter of interest. Our history shapes us. As Alcoff (2015: 56) says:

> History doesn't excuse us, but it explains the conditions in which the inter-
> pretive process is occurring: what concepts I have at my disposal, how I am
> positioned vis- à- vis the 'deep rules' of my milieu, and, most importantly,
> what of my own history is at stake as I try to make sense of new events.

There is no starting place for this history as I am sure that human beings have always divided the world into 'us' and 'them', probably since before Neanderthals were wiped out and when Britain's 'Cheddar man' lived about 10,000 years ago (who was found, through his DNA, to have very dark skin and blue eyes (The Guardian, 2018)). I will start my history of whiteness with the Ancient Greeks, Romans and other European tribes, though, as there is more documented about their times. From this period, I will travel through time to the present day, briefly documenting the historical events that influence our lives today.

Ancient Romans and Greeks

The idea that humankind is divided into different 'peoples'[1] goes back to a remote past. The Romans travelled to distant lands and so gave names to the groups of peoples they found. Differences in culture were often accounted for by differences in climate as they regarded their own climate as perfect – neither too hot nor too cold (Irvin Painter, 2010). The Greeks used this idea as a way of justifying their superiority (Kendi, 2016:17). This, no doubt, helped them to distinguish themselves from other groups and justified attacking and subjugating them. The colour of the skin of different tribes or groups had no meaning for them, though other characteristics were described, such as how war-like or brave they were. The term 'race' was not coined until the late 16th century to denote a 'people' and not used in a quasi-scientific way as an ethnicity until the 18th century (Hannaford, 1996:14).

The peoples described by the Romans include, for instance, the Scythians (present day Iranians), the Germani (Germans) and the Gauls (French) (Irvin Painter, 2010). Aristeas, reported by Herodotus, confidently describes monstrous people such as the Arimaspi from Scythia, who had one eye in the middle of their forehead, and a group that had no hair from childhood and could see better at night than during the day (Irvin Painter, 2010). Herodotus's description of other Scythian's as having cannibalistic tendencies seems to call into question his reliable knowledge, having heard those portrayals! Julius Caesar also leaves us with some descriptions of different peoples. He describes the Brits as people who dressed in skins and dyed their bodies blue with woad to give them a more frightening appearance in battle (Irvin Painter, 2010). We do not know for sure why or if they dyed their bodies blue – it could have been for decorative purposes. Apart from the fact that it is unlikely that woad was used in this way, as it would not be easy to dye the human body with it, it is almost certainly conjecture on Julius Caesar's part to say that it was to make them look frightening (Irvin Painter, 2010). It may say more about how he felt when faced with the Brits than their motivation for dyeing their bodies in this way. The idea of ferocious, blue-painted ancient Brits has come down to us in the public imagination, much in the way that the idea of black people having a

---

1   I will use Corry's definition of a 'people', which is 'an identifiable society' (Corry 2011:91)

good sense of rhythm has come down to white people and is an example of how concepts about other cultures can become lodged in the popular imagination.

Most descriptions of other peoples, though, have come to us through the writings of those who were not part of the group. This gives them a quasi-objective feel – much like the scholarly writings of anthropologists later in the 19th and 20th centuries such as Samuel George Morton, who was obsessed with the differences between the skulls of different races. He thought these indicated characteristics like intelligence (Irvin Painter, 2010). This will be discussed below in more detail.

It seems that human beings have long engaged in constructing simple, generalised ideas about 'other' groups, maybe to make the world more predictable and understandable. They also, from ancient days, have tended to create hierarchies in which some groups (usually the ones describing the hierarchy) were superior to others (Kendi, 2016). In fact, the Greeks regarded climate as an important factor in making them superior. As we saw above, they regarded themselves as neither too hot nor too cool. As a forerunner of opinions held much closer to our own times, Aristotle thought the way that the climate creates pale or dark skins (he thought that African skin was 'burnt') was evidence of this and justified the Greeks holding slaves (Kendi, 2016).

When the term 'white' was first coined to denote people of Europe and the term 'race' invented, there was a desire to find a valid history for the origins of this 'race' (Irvin Painter, 2010). Greece and Rome were looked to as progenitors, and the idealised sculptures of Greek and Roman statues were seen as providing a gratifyingly beautiful and white image. We now know that these statues, made of white marble, were in fact painted to look life-like and that Ancient Greeks and Romans were almost certainly brown skinned (Irvin Painter, 2016). It is interesting that Shakespeare, well after the fall of Greece and Rome, wrote of contemporary Italians but also of more northerly historical figures, placing them in their national context, such as Macbeth, in Scotland; Hamlet, in Denmark; and King Lear, who was Celtic. Later, the Anglo Saxons were turned to as our forebears, as we will see below.

Post-Roman Europe

Later, in what became known as the 'Dark Ages' when the Romans had left Europe, the term 'Saxon' appears to denote people who invaded Britain and were mostly from Germany and Denmark, including Angles and Jutes, sometimes later called Anglo Saxons (Alcoff, 2015; Irvin Painter, 2010). These people fought between themselves and also against the Vikings who made conquests throughout northern Europe. Although Africans were present in large numbers in Greece and Rome as well as in Roman Europe generally, Africa was not visited by northern Europeans at this time or vice versa.

By the 11th century, the theatre of warfare increased, particularly as Pope Urban II called for a crusade against the Muslims in order to reclaim the Holy Land. Many young men set out for Palestine as a religious act to promote Christianity. The greatest differentiator between peoples had, by then, become religion rather than race. The hatred of other people therefore turned more to Muslims and Jews. Although the crusaders would have met black people from North Africa, their religion was more an issue for them than their colour. No doubt this hatred of non-Christian religions, which ran deep at the time, has simmered, more-or-less under the surface since then. It can emerge as anti-Semitism and more recently as Islamophobia.

Although religion has been a catalyst for conflict throughout the ages, there have been times of remarkable peace and appreciation between the different groups, particularly in the 10th and 11th centuries in places like Cordoba and Andalucia when Christians, Jews and Muslims lived together in great harmony. In Spain, this was known as the La Convivencia as these different religious groups shared their knowledge and wisdom generously. Although this is sometimes cynically said to be exaggerated, it was certainly better than the persecution that followed when, in the late 15th century, Jews and Muslims were either killed, expelled or made to convert to Roman Catholicism. This was the time of the Spanish Inquisition, which started in 1478 and did not end until 1834. The 10th, 11th and 12th centuries also saw much global travel and interchange of philosophy, science and mathematics. For instance, Adelard of Bath (my home town) travelled extensively throughout the Mediterranean and the Middle East. He learned Arabic and could therefore understand Arabic mathematics including Euclid's geometry, which had been lost in Greek but was translated into Arabic. He made various translations from the Arabic into Latin, thereby making this knowledge accessible to western countries, leading to their ability to build the great cathedrals of that time, including Chartres in France and Wells in England. This ushered in the Renaissance in the West which drew on the Islamic Golden Age, a fact not often acknowledged (Cockrane, 1994).

Racism in Europe

It is interesting that the histories of the 'white race' in the USA and Europe have many differences though each influenced the other's ideas and scholarship (Irvin Painter, 2010). Their histories are related because white Americans originated in Europe and the slave trade was a collaboration between Europe and the Americas. Nevertheless, in order to make things clearer, I will explore these separately.

The history of Europe in regard to black people starts surprisingly early. We know that black people from Ethiopia and other parts of Africa were well known to Ancient Romans and Greeks and many were enslaved (Kendi, 2016). However, it became increasingly common to see black faces in Europe when explorers sailed out from various nations in the 15th century, looking originally for adventures and for new goods to trade (Uloso, 2016). They were often motivated by wanting to see new things and have novel experiences. Trading far from home must have required great courage, and been exciting as well as lucrative. Spices from the Far East, for instance, were much prized and the ancient trade route of the Silk Road was used to bring these and other goods from China (Menzies, 2016).

Besides bringing wondrous goods to sell, such explorers would tell breathtaking tales of extraordinary sights – many of which were very fanciful – describing that which lay beyond the land so far discovered. Maps of the time would have pictures of fabulous creatures where the limits of present knowledge ran out. Human beings that were to be found far from Europe also seemed strange and exciting, with apparently outlandish and bizarre habits and appearances. They were seen in much the same way as the exotic animals and plants found in distant lands. Sometimes people brought specimens home, including human beings. These unfortunate people often died of diseases such as influenza or measles as they had no immunity against them (Irvin Painter, 2010). Wanchese, for example, was a famous Native American who was introduced to the King of England and other important people in 1584, a sight to be wondered at. It is often thought (Uloso, 2016) that the history of black people in Europe started in the 20th century but, in fact, there is historical evidence that many black people lived and worked there, albeit with some notable exceptions, at the lower end of society, many centuries before that (Uloso, 2016).

Colonisation

As more was discovered in far-away lands, it became clear that, if the different European countries were to make the most of trading opportunities, they would have to annex these lands so that they could claim the trade for themselves rather than share with other European countries. A rush to appropriate colonies proceeded in the 15th century when the Portuguese colonised Ceuta in North Africa in 1415.

Many European nations conquered parts of the rest of the world which could not yet, of course, be called countries – it was Europeans who drew these boundaries and gave them names. The mores of the time were such that this was entirely without shame and there was even the view that they were doing the people they found there a favour by ruling them and bringing European 'civilisation'. This importantly included Christianity, and was a major part of that justification (Henry, 2007). The confidence and arrogance to hold these beliefs went without challenge for centuries.

In fact, colonisation has brought with it untold and lasting conflict between different peoples who lived on the land eventually sequestered by Europeans. It forced different peoples with different cultural identities to form a country together (Corry, 2011). This was exacerbated by the colonising authorities choosing one tribe to become dominant over another by giving them authority to administer the colony. A tribe whose members' appearance had a more European 'look' was usually chosen. This set the seeds for even greater conflict such as that between Hutus and Tutsis which lasts to this day in Ruanda and Burundi. Although many centuries have passed, the tensions between different tribes remain and cause conflict that is hard, if not impossible, to resolve. There are also peoples who have been split by the artificial borders running between them, forcing them to become different nations. They often long to be reunited as one country. These include the Kurds and the Tamils. This situation causes untold suffering through the subjugation of peoples and the bloody conflicts which have been generated by colonial interference. This is particularly true of the uneasy relationship between Kurds and the majority who live in the countries they inhabit. Kurds have been divided, by the British, between four different countries: Iran, Iraq, Syria and Turkey. Now each of these countries will not countenance Kurds being given their own homeland, and this has resulted in their subjugation and bloody conflict.

When, in the 18th and 19th centuries, colonisation was at its height and explorers were sailing out from European countries to places such as Africa and the Caribbean, the idea of the European as the 'white' man grew up. When it was first used, the term 'race' meant nation or ethnic group but later acquired its present meaning with connotations of scientifically proven hierarchy between races (Kendi, 2016). By the 19th century, the 'white man' was seen, not only as 'civilised', intelligent and capable, he (sic) was understood to have almost a duty of care towards the 'black' man – at least in Britain – as exemplified in this poem called *Song of the White Men* by Rudyard Kipling written in 1899:

Now, this is the cup the White Men drink
     When they go to right a wrong,
And that is the cup of the old world's hate –
     Cruel and strained and strong.
We have drunk that cup – and a bitter, bitter cup –
     And tossed the dregs away.
But well for the world when the White Men drink
     To the dawn of the White Man's day!

Now, this is the road that the White Men tread
     When they go to clean a land –
Iron underfoot and levin[2] overhead
     And the deep on either hand.

We have trod that road – and a wet and windy road –
     Our chosen star for guide.
Oh, well for the world when the White Men tread
     Their highway side by side!

---

2   Thunderbolts

Now, this is the faith that the White Men hold –
   When they build their homes afar –
'Freedom for ourselves and freedom for our sons
   And, failing freedom, War.'

We have proved our faith – bear witness to our faith,
   Dear souls of freemen slain!
Oh, well for the world when the White Men join
   To prove their faith again!

Of all the European countries, Britain established the most colonies and built up a huge empire which lasted well into the 20th century. A map of the world famously looked pink as all the British colonies had that colour. It was said that the sun never set on the British Empire. I well remember looking proudly at a map of the world when I was a small child in the 1950s and being told that the pink bits were the British Empire. It then seemed entirely natural.

In 1875, the term 'Caucasian race' was invented by the German philosopher Christof Meiners and taken up by Johann Friedrich Blumenbach, who became the father of anthropology. They were concerned to make a taxonomy of different races such as Caucasian, Mongoloid and Negroid. The Caucasians were held to be people of remarkable beauty and more intelligent and capable (Alcoff, 2015; Baum, 2008). That which constituted human beauty became a scientific preoccupation at the time and the Caucasian race was considered to be the epitome. This set the scene for, and excused, the dominance of white people over others. Later the term 'Caucasian' was used as a term for 'white' or European and is still sometimes used today, lending the idea of whiteness a certain spurious scientific validity (Baum, 2008).

From the point of view of European colonisation, race has been an important construct which coalesced into two races: black and white. The whites were the colonisers and the blacks the colonised. In the 18th and 19th centuries, black people were generally seen as little more than animals (Cambell & Oakes, 1998) who could be bought and sold at will as slaves and treated as beasts in the way that they were transported and packed like sardines in a tin.

In the 21st century, we are beginning to understand that animals should not in any case be treated disrespectfully and without considering their dignity and comfort. Even those who worked to abolish slavery did not really see black people as sentient human beings, and those who advocated its abolition tended to treat slaves in the way that people interested in animal welfare would treat animals in the 20th century (Kendi, 2016). Slaves were sometimes seen as being like children who were naturally 'happy and docile' but 'inherently weak and childlike'(Kendi, 2016: 193). In America (to which we soon turn) they were seen either as a 'Sambo' who was happy and docile or a 'Nat', named after a rebellious slave called Nat Turner (Kendi, 2016). His name has been used to refer to the slave who turned against his master and became 'disobedient and aggressive' (Frederickson, 1997).

Europeans became very rich on the slave trade and the wealth of many of their cities are based on it. In the UK, for instance, Bristol, Bath and Liverpool were very prosperous indeed and many of the great mansions in the UK were built with this money. It is rarely recognised, for instance, that great mansions now owned by the British National Trust were built by people who became wealthy because of the slave trade. We clearly still benefit to this day from the blood money of that time.

The United States of America

White Americans, along with Australians, New Zealanders and Canadians, had originally been European colonisers who had all but wiped out the people who had been living in those countries until they arrived (Corry, 2011). The brutality and heartless indifference with which this entirely self-serving act was carried out seems to be beyond our ability to thoroughly own. The subsequent enslavement of black people in America was equally merciless. The idea that the USA was the 'land of the free', which gave refuge to all persecuted people and that those who wanted to better themselves were welcome, was mostly a myth. Which people should be allowed into the country was the preoccupation of many, including intellectuals and academics, who were interested in race, particularly when people from outside northern Europe started to knock on the door. This included the Irish escaping famine caused and exacerbated by British policies. In America, the Irish were, for decades, treated very badly and, in many instances, treated much like slaves (Kendi, 2016). Eastern Europeans were also reviled, particularly Jewish people, who were escaping pogroms in Russia. Other eastern European countries that were part of the pre-Soviet Russian Empire were also not welcome, as well as southern Europeans, especially impoverished Italians, looking for a better life. Although their skin colour was mostly indistinguishable from northern Europeans, eastern and southern Europeans were not really considered white (Jacobson, 1998). In order to try to find a rationale for excluding these people from America, race-based theories were adopted. At that time, African slaves were almost considered to be outside the concept of race altogether, rather in the way that homeless people today are regarded as being part of an underclass – not even dignified with belonging to a class at all (Savage, 2015).

Eminent citizens like Ralph Waldo Emerson, a much-respected essayist and poet and generally known for his liberal and abolitionist views, urged the government to restrict emigration to America to 'Anglo Saxons'. The views of Emerson, who was a Unitarian, Transcendentalist, philosopher and Dean of Harvard, show how white dominance became mainstream and was even promulgated by people who are even now considered people of substance. Although he rejected the worst of the racist thinking of the time and was an advocate of the abolition of slavery (Irvin Painter, 2010), his views are very shocking today. Indeed, I find this particularly shocking myself as I had regarded him as a man with wisdom and humanity, as expressed in his other writings. I only came across what he wrote about race when researching material for this book. I mention him particularly here as, for me, it shows how utterly 'normal' racist ideas were in America at the time, even among apparently enlightened people.

In 1850, Emerson wrote in his diary that the black man 'is created on a lower plane than the white, and eats men and kidnaps and tortures if he can. The Negro is reactionary merely in his successes and there is no origination with him in mental and moral sphere' (Emerson, 1977:280). At the same time, his pride in being of English stock led him to describe New Englanders as being 'double distilled English' (Nicholoff, 1994:xxi). This typified the attitude of erudite academics and politicians to other 'races' such as the Irish and eastern Europeans, and is very shocking by today's standards. For instance, in 1851 Emerson likened other races to 'guano' which was a fertiliser made from bird excrement. He said, 'The German and Irish have a deal of guano in their destiny. They are ferried over the Atlantic, and carted over America to ditch and to drudge, to make the land fertile, and corn cheap and then to lie down prematurely to make the grass a spot of greener grass on the prairie' (Emerson, 1975:60). In other words, if they come into the country it is to make it habitable for the whites. In 1829, he showed what he thought of black people, as well as those from other races, when he wrote:

> I think it cannot be maintained by any candid person that the African race have ever occupied or do promise ever to occupy any very high place in the human family. Their present condition is the strongest proof that they cannot. The Irish cannot; the American Indian cannot; the Chinese cannot. Before the energy of the Caucasian race all the other races have quailed and so done obeisance. (Emerson, 1977)

The Irish were often likened to black people, particularly in their poverty caused by the potato famine and seen, like those from other 'inferior' races, as being unsuited to being given the vote (Irvin Painter, 2010). Unsurprisingly, the Irish themselves tended to be against abolishing slavery as their place in American society was at least one better than that of slaves. It seems surprising now that the Irish were held in slave-like conditions. I came across white people from Barbados who said they were descended from Irish slaves. Though there is some controversy about whether they were slaves or indentured labourers, they lived in very harsh conditions and were there against their will. This confirms both that the Irish were considered to be like black people and that the Irish themselves did not want to be considered this way and drew a line between themselves and black slaves.

From this we can see that the fundamental idea of 'white' superiority was built on centuries of race prejudice and was now being re-formed and confirmed as America created the foundations of its country. As Alcoff says:

> Projections of inferiority on the groups unjustly treated by whites then serves the helpful purpose of explaining away racist violence, softening the sense of guilt, and legitimating the legacies of unequal distributions that whites enjoy today. (Alcoff, 2015:83)

We can see that the notion of whiteness was restricted to what was thought of as Anglo Saxon, which in practice was northern European but was particularly English. At the same time, emigration to America from southern and eastern Europe was growing, as well as from Ireland. Later, towards the end of the 19th century, the Irish began to be accepted as northern Europeans and therefore 'became white' (Alcoff, 2015:12). Another New Englander, Francis Amasa Walker, an economist, statistician, journalist, educator and military officer, bemoaned the arrival of new immigrants who, he said, came from:

> so broad and smooth a channel, [that] there is no reason why every foul and stagnant pool of population in Europe, which no breath of intellectual or industrial life has stirred for ages, should not be decanted upon our soil. Hard times here may momentarily check the flow; but it will not be permanently stopped so long as any difference of economic level exists between our population and that of the most degraded communities abroad. (Walker, 1896:822)

These views can be found today with, for example, the refugee crisis, though not expressed so readily.

Extraordinary lengths were taken to show, in a quasi-scientific way, the superiority of Anglo Saxon (or Teutonic) peoples and the inferiority of other 'races' such as Celts, Alpines and Mediterraneans (Alcoff, 2015:94; Irvin Painter, 2010). As mentioned above, much time and energy was given to the measurement of skulls. Tectonics were supposed to be 'dolichocephalic' or long headed and blond, while others were 'brachycephalic' (round headed) and dark (Irvin Painter, 2010). This way of thinking seems to prefigure Hitler's understanding of race. Walker wrote an addendum to cover Jews but found that they tended to be like the people in areas where they live so did not see them as a separate 'race' but as a 'people'.

This is a very short description of the convoluted study made of races in America but it gives some idea of the way in which 'whiteness' was seen at the time. It was, from their point of view, the pinnacle of human superiority. The makeup of the white race seemed to change over time as different nationalities fell within its definition. It would be tempting to think that the people from northern states of the USA were not as prejudiced as slave-owning southerners, as the Civil War was largely fought over the issue of slavery. However, whatever their motivation for wanting to ban slavery, it did not come from the idea that we are all 'born equal' in the way we would mean it today, as can be seen from the kinds of views expressed by northerners like Emerson above.

Views about race, such as these, persisted into the 20th century, with authors extolling the greatness of the white race which had been given various other names to distinguish it from inferior whites. The name 'Nordic' to name a superior white person was used by Madison Grant, for instance (Spiro, 2009), who wanted to keep the race 'pure' through eugenics. The Klu Klux Klan arose in three different time periods (1860–70 and 1915–20) and again in the 1950s, when it formed to oppose the Civil Rights Movement. It is a secret society, with members protected by robes which hide their faces. Their agenda is to promote the 'purity' of the white race (Kendi, 2016).

The 20th century in Europe and America

It is often said that the Second World War was borne from Germany being disgraced and severely humiliated when it lost the First World War (Taylor, 2001). Maybe Germans needed to refind a sense of pride in their identity. The idea of a pure 'Arian' race (yet another word for the white race) was proposed by Hitler and readily taken up by the German people. Jews were seen as a corrupting influence on the purity of the race and therefore should be exterminated. This led, as is well known, to the Jewish Holocaust in which over five million Jews were killed in concentration camps along with Roma, Slavs and Poles, who were also considered to be polluting the race. Maybe this devastatingly shocking event has served as a wake-up call for Germany and the rest of the white world, as the idea of a 'pure' race holds, at least consciously, less credibility in general now, though it can still emerge as a compelling idea to some extremists from time to time and is expressed, typically, by people belonging to far-right political parties.

After the Second World War, there was a move to give self-rule to colonies. There may be several reasons why European countries acquiesced to this demand, mostly, no doubt, economic, but maybe also because a post-war moral justification for owning them became untenable. Following the dismantling of the British Empire, the British Commonwealth of Nations was established in 1949 and residents of ex-colonies were given the right to come to the UK freely. While this could be characterised as a way of encouraging ex-colonies to keep good relationships with the UK, there was greater self-interest involved, as there was a large shortage of people to take jobs to rebuild the country after the war. Many took advantage of this situation and came to find work and improve their standard of living for themselves and their families. The *HMT Empire Windrush*, which set sail from Jamaica in 1948, was one of the first boats to arrive with those seeking employment in Britain (Uloso, 2016). In spite of Caribbean people taking on much-needed employment, there was a now infamous antipathy towards them. Finding accommodation was hard and signs saying 'No blacks, no Irish, no Dogs' were said to be rife (Eddo-Lodge, 2017). There is some doubt about how common this actually was, but the sentiment behind it was certainly present among the British population. Jamaicans were the vanguard of large numbers of people from many Commonwealth countries who have now settled in Britain – bringing with them different cultural habits and customs, including music, food and family patterns that help to make UK cities so vibrant and multicultural.

As in many other European countries, there has been an ambivalent response to this new situation. Many white people objected to those who looked different and had different ways coming into their towns and cities. Race has been a preoccupation for the British over the last six or so decades. There have been politicians who ramped up anti-black feeling such as the British conservative politician, Enoch Powell, with his famous 'rivers of blood' speech (Eddo-Lodge, 2017; Uloso, 2016). In it he warned that there would inevitably be violence on the street unless immigration was curbed. Other politicians have tried to encourage a multicultural society which involved a peaceful co-existence with different communities.

The Race Relations Act became law in 1965 and banned 'discrimination on the grounds of colour, race or ethnic or national origins' in public places. In 1968, it was strengthened to include employment and housing. Both of these laws occurred during the tenure of a Labour government who, under the influence of campaigners and professionals who worked with disadvantaged groups (Dominelli, 2006a), spearheaded a more tolerant attitude to those from non-British races and cultures. In the European Union, the extensive

European Convention on Human Rights was adopted in 1953, although it has been amended several times since then. Many opposed to Britain leaving the European Union fear that the rights of UK citizens will be affected by losing the protection of this law. In America, the Civil Rights Movement, which exists to end racial discrimination of all kinds, was successful in securing certain civil rights by law in America. The Civil Rights Act was passed in 1964, the Voting Rights Act in 1965 and the Fair Housing act in 1968. This did not by any means put an end to racial prejudice as we will see below.

From 1960 to 1990 Britain became increasingly multicultural. The new, more tolerant attitude was, to some extent, successful and the 1990s saw an increase in the number of black people entering middle-class jobs and becoming successful, particularly second and third generation black British (Olusoga, 2016). Black people became more and more confident in asserting their right to equality and to practise and display their cultural heritage within the panoply of different cultures in the British Isles. This tolerance of difference was only partial, however, and there were many disturbances and conflicts on the way.

The growth of the Notting Hill carnival was a case in point. I, with my husband and baby, were caught up with the riots in 1978 as we lived close to the streets where the carnival passed. It was a magnificent parade and party atmosphere but towards the evening, policemen, who had been bussed in from other forces all over Britain and were cooped up in coaches all day, were let out into the streets and responded harshly to carnival goers. Black people were 'kettled' and then attacked, while I and my family, along with other whites, were made to go in a different direction, away from trouble. Later we watched as police chased young black men through our garden. The following year we noticed the police going into the school opposite our flat. My husband went to talk to them and asked how they were going to avoid the problems of the previous year. It was through this conversation we heard that the police had previously been held in coaches. This year they were taken to a school where they could play badminton and other games and have refreshments. They were then sent into the festival, a few at a time, where they could join in with the fun. The occasion passed off peacefully that year and has more or less done so ever since. This was at a time when, with the Labour government, there was a certain amount of political will to improve race relations, but racist attitudes persisted. Brixton, another largely black area, was also known for its riots. Both areas have become gentrified since then and have been taken over by people who can afford the inflated house prices.

In spite of progress made at this time, a general acceptance that racism is 'wrong' and some progress made in black people becoming more integrated into society, this only goes so far. Compared with their numbers in the population, there are more black people in poverty-stricken areas (Savage, 2015) and fewer represented on, for instance, boards of corporations, the House of Commons, the professions and the arts. Black people are also much more likely to be stopped and searched by police (Eddo-Lodge, 2017). StopWatch, an organisation set up to address concerns about the use of stop and search tactics by police, has reported that black people were four times more likely to be stopped and searched than whites in London in 2016/17 (StopWatch, 2018). Black people are also overrepresented in prisons and mental hospitals (Eddo-Lodge, 2017). All these matters have recently been discussed in the media as I write in 2018. It seems that white people will only go so far to give up their privilege.

In the 1980s, the term 'politically correct' came into use in Europe and America to describe the avoidance of language and behaviour that denigrates disadvantaged people, particularly those of different races (Delahanty, 2011). The term has an ambivalent connotation. Some may use it as a serious injunction to encourage non-prejudiced behaviour while others use it ironically and mockingly. With the turn to racial integration that was becoming more acceptable in the 1970s and 80s, it was generally considered not good form to be discovered in prejudiced actions and behaviours so that those who worked in public services such as the police were taught the language that was 'politically correct', but it tended to change minds rather than hearts. For instance, a very revealing BBC documentary (Carter, 2003) showed, through the use of hidden cameras held by an undercover reporter, how police would display very racist attitudes when they thought that they were not in the public gaze. A more recent documentary which used hidden recording equipment showed similar behaviour of staff in an immigration detention centre, though it did not mention whether or not the staff there had any training in race or cultural awareness. There is a more in-depth exploration concerning political correctness in Chapter 3.

Post 2016

In 2016, we saw:

- the British decide to leave the European Union, which came to be known as Brexit, in an in–out referendum
- Donald Trump, a right-wing populist Republican, elected to be President of the United States of America
- other populist, right-wing parties in Europe either gaining power or greatly increasing their share of the vote.

The extent to which a large proportion of the public in these countries, mostly, but not entirely, white, seemed to feel under siege from foreigners was thus revealed. In the British case particularly, having to abide by European laws about free movement of people within the Union was a huge issue and gained momentum when eastern European countries joined the European Union and were thus able to freely come to live and work in the UK. A desire to 'take control of our borders' was one of the clarion calls of those who voted to leave the European Union. This occurred at a time when the numbers of refugees trying to enter the UK and other European nations was rocketing. Refugees desperately trying to find safety, some walking in long lines, some perilously crowded into small boats and others trying frantically to get into the backs of lorries in Calais, were constantly on our screens. Calls for limiting the numbers of refugees allowed into each country were very loud and generally accepted by all political parties. Angela Merkel's generosity (and no doubt self-interest in the need for low-paid workers) was striking in taking nearly one million refugees in 2015. There has been a backlash in her party since then. The issues that gave rise to these events are complex. Here are some of them.

Globalisation

First, there is the issue of globalisation, which is criticised by both the right and the left wing. Those on the right wing think that globalisation results in their national identity being watered down and not protected by government. With globalisation comes greater mobility, leading to fears that towns and villages will be 'swamped' by foreigners who look different and have different habits and customs. Many feel that immigrants destroy the smooth running of society and compete for amenities in the community, often, in their view, being given services before those who have lived in the country for generations. The left wing is critical of globalisation because of the way that huge multinational corporations become very rich on the backs of ordinary people and leave others impoverished. The issue of manufacturing jobs being taken from western workers and carried out in 'developing' countries is also an issue, particularly for trade unions.

Multiculturalism

Some 'progressive' people of most European and American countries, in the second half of the 20th century, advocated 'multiculturalism' as a policy for ensuring peaceful diverse communities. This policy, which was never officially a policy at all but generally thought of as correct by most policy makers, involved encouraging black and minority ethnic groups to follow their own customs while also being part of the larger community. Their customs were often considered to be an enriching contribution to society and many people enjoyed the cultural mix. This idea can be criticised because it assumes that it is possible for different cultures to co-exist happily where racist power dynamics are present (Dominelli, 2006b). Courses in multiculturalism were sometimes promoted instead of anti-racist courses as they seemed to be less subversive (Eddo-Lodge, 2017). Although there was some, maybe unaware, racism involved in multiculturalism, it did at least acknowledge that multiple cultural groups within society can be enriching for the whole.

Since the turn of the millennium, multiculturalism has become more and more criticised on other grounds – that it is a failed policy for ensuring peaceful communities and is blamed for the upsurge in terrorist activities (Lennon, 2016). It has been argued in the UK that black and minority ethnic (BME) communities have been too inward looking and have not been integrated into mainstream society. This is contrasted with American policy, where communities are encouraged to identify with being American before the culture of their heritage (Lennon, 2016). While it is true that Islamic-inspired terrorism is on the increase in the UK, this has many causes but not, I think, because society has been too tolerant of cultural expression. The alienation of these communities from the mainstream is much more likely to be the cause and this is certainly not within the spirit of multiculturalism. So, while it may be true that communities that are isolated from British society may lead to disaffected people, this is only the case if they feel that they have no place in the wider community and there is no way of individuals and groups making a truly meaningful and successful life for themselves.

I have written more about multiculturalism in Chapter 7. In any case, following the American example and explicitly encouraging an identification with Britain before that of their country of origin country is, I feel, unlikely to succeed. Explicit expression of patriotism is not common in Britain and may not sit easily within British culture. Overt expressions of attachment to the place of one's birth are not common but that does not mean they do not exist. Even a Londoner who comes to live in a British village or small town would not be accepted as being 'from' there, even if they had been living there for 30 years and taken part in every village fete all that time! Even their children who were born and bred there may struggle to be accepted as really belonging. (I know this to be true as I have experienced this very scenario!) The same applies to immigrants – many generations have to pass before they are accepted as 'one of us'. Black people are often asked where they come from, the assumption being that they are not from 'here'. Nevertheless, the American example of encouraging identification with America before that of the original country has not led to racial harmony, even if America does have less Islamic terrorism in spite of having a very large Muslim community. This could be because of draconian anti-Islamic practices in immigration and policing. The price for this has probably not yet been paid in mid-2018.

Hostile attitudes to foreigners in general seem to have been unleashed in the UK since the Brexit referendum and have given licence to xenophobic attitudes that would previously have been frowned on. Populist politicians who 'say it as it is', such as Nigel Farage and Boris Johnson, have become popular. It was as if many people had been holding their breath and walking on eggs shells until the referendum gave permission to breathe deeply and smash the eggs shells by expressing feelings of antipathy to foreigners (Irvin Painter, 2016).

This atmosphere of hostility to migrants has resulted in the government devising a policy to make it more difficult for migrants to enter Britain, which has become known as a 'hostile environment' policy (Elgot, 2018). This hostile environment has affected many people who have previously migrated to Britain as well as people entering the UK, including those escaping persecution. It has also led to people who have been living in Britain legally for decades being threatened with deportation, including what has become known in the press as the 'Windrush generation', who were not given papers at the time of their immigration and have difficulty proving that they have a right to live and work in Britain.

A similar sentiment was revealed at the same time in the USA with the election of Donald Trump. He characterised himself as representing ordinary people who had been much put upon by the 'establishment' in the past. Those who voted for him in large numbers were white but not necessarily, as is popularly thought, working class (Coates, 2017:345). They were, though, angry about the decline of America's global economic supremacy. It seemed that at last they were being listened to and represented. One of Trump's rallying cries was 'America first!' by which one might hear 'White America first!' and 'Make America Great Again' for which one might hear 'Make White People Great Again' – thus diverting the blame for economic woes on to foreigners. He was famously upbraided for shortsighted environmental policies as well as protectionist and nationalistic policies by President Macron of France when he spoke to both the House of Representatives and the Senate. He used the phrases 'make the planet great again' and 'there is no planet B'.

We must not therefore overplay the numbers of people holding these views. Trump did not win the popular vote and 48 per cent of the people who voted in the UK referendum voted for Remain, but it showed that the discontent of white people about racial integration and losing their privileged place in the world is considerable. These issues will be looked at in more detail in subsequent chapters as well as an exploration given of more effective ways of tackling the global inequality spearheaded by white supremacy. The historian Ibram X Kendi (2016), writing in his book, *Stamped from the Beginning: The Definitive History of Racist Ideas in America*, shows how neither the optimistic nor the pessimistic narratives are useful. The optimistic being: 'things are getting better' as exemplified by anti-discrimination laws and the election of Barack Obama to the Presidency of the United States, and the pessimistic being the chronic occurrence of poverty and systematic mistreatment by the authorities of black people. Neither helps us to understand interracial dynamics.

As in the UK and other places in Europe, we seem to swing between the two ends of this spectrum. Maybe we will continue to see this swinging from one pole to the other while government policies do not take the majority of the population with them in building healthy and tolerant societies. Being accused of racism leads to shame, but undigested shame does not lead to a change in attitude as it either goes underground or emerges in anger and aggression. We need to find ways of changing hearts as well as minds to effect any lasting change, not only about racism as such, but also about white privilege and how a more equal world will lead to a more peaceful and prosperous one (Jaccobson-Widding, 1979). There will be more on this in Chapter 10.

The ecological crisis

The ecological crisis is another factor to add to the effects of white supremacy over the centuries. Indigenous peoples, on the whole, lived and still live, in great harmony with nature and understand themselves to be an integral part of the natural world (Corry, 2011). The idea that we can exploit nature, nevertheless, has ancient roots, in that the Torah and the Christian Old Testament say that we have dominion over the plants and animals (Genesis 1:26). This idea did not gather pace until the Industrial Revolution made it possible to exploit the resources of the earth much more thoroughly. Nature seemed limitless and ours for the taking. The way that white neoliberalism has contributed disastrously to the acceleration of the pace of this exploitation is explored more fully in Chapter 8.

Many of the themes of this history will be taken up and explored in further chapters of this book. This chapter, though longer than the others, is the basis on which all the rest stand. We start with looking in depth at the way in which we are still privileged as white people today and how that rests on the history outlined above.

CHAPTER 3

How Are White People Privileged?

I n this chapter, we will explore the way in which white history as outlined in the last chapter still haunts us today. Two effects stem from our history and mean that we cannot shake it off. In spite of this, it is often regarded as something that is not relevant to us today. These two effects are:

1. We are still living off the proceeds of colonisation, exploitation and slavery from the past.
2. Our attitudes to non-white people are shaped by our history and imbued with attitudes from those times, even when we think they are not.

These facts are not easy to come to terms with as they imply a guilt that is not easily understood or responded to. Some people are angered by these ideas, particularly if they are not rich or powerful and feel they are the victims of exploitation themselves. Some may think that non-white people get preferential treatment or point to rich and successful black people who seem to give the lie to white privilege. Nevertheless, taken more generally, white people are much richer and more powerful than they would have been if the trajectory of history had not taken the course of colonisation that it did. I will show in Chapter 4 that, although there are ways in which society disadvantages other groups (such as working-class, gay, disabled people, etc.), insofar as they are white, they do still benefit.

So, what are the benefits and privileges I am referring to? I have organised them into seven areas for clarity. They are being 'just normal'; political and economic arrangements; building on past wealth; the building of Britain's great cities; the supremacy of the English language; style of dress; and white sport.

Being 'just normal'

As we saw in Chapter 1, history in western societies is very much told from a white standpoint. This gives white people a view of themselves as being 'just normal' (Dyer, 1997; Ryde, 2009) while others 'have' a culture, race and colour. Frankenberg (1999:16) called white people 'the unmarked marker of others'. White people invented the term 'race' and named the races. Dyer (1997: 14) pointed out that 'there is no more powerful position than being 'just' normal'. White people's societal arrangements take precedence worldwide and are the standard by which others are judged.

This apparent normality has allowed white people to be unthinkingly self-confident about their position in the world and the rightness of their cultural arrangements. Irvin Painter points out that, from early in the mid-19th century, '[white] racial superiority now permeated concepts of race in the United States and virtually throughout the English-speaking world' (Irvin Painter, 2010).

It is interesting that, originating in the 'Cold War' when communism was pitted against the West, the West divided the world into the first, second and third world. It went without saying that the West was the first world, being self-evidently most powerful and the envy of others who wished to emulate it.

Building on past wealth

Within the capitalist system, past wealth is the capital we use to build further prosperity. Britain became very wealthy, particularly in the 18th and 19th centuries, and this wealth flowed from the colonies where commodities such as cotton, sugar, tea, gold, silver and other natural resources were discovered, appropriated and exported to Europe. Slaves were used to carry out this difficult, dangerous, exhausting and laborious work as well as infrastructure development, which ensured that products could be transported. The triangular slave trade, which was particularly lucrative and efficient, was the means by which sufficient numbers of slaves were found to carry out this work. Slaves cruelly captured, wrenched from their families and communities were taken from Africa to the Americas and the West Indies where they were sold to white landowners; their place in the ships was then taken by raw materials such as cotton and sugar that were carried from America to Britain where they were manufactured into saleable goods and then transported to Africa where they were sold. Money was made at each point of the triangle and the ships did not have to travel at any point with only ballast in their hold. The riches made in this and other ways of exploiting the potential wealth of colonies, hugely benefited the British nation as a whole – as well as individual families. These riches are still with us today.

Tate and Lyle, for example, were sugar importers from the West Indies. They were Quakers who espoused ethical values and had high (for the times) standards for their British workers' living conditions. Although the company did not start until slaves had been emancipated, their wealth was built on the notorious sugar trade and employment practices were still exploitative after slavery. The slaves did not have much choice but to continue in the same place of work after the abolition of slavery but with poverty wages where the notorious 'apprenticeship' labour system forced them to stay with their former employers (Heuman, 2000). Tate and Lyle made vast profits from which the company still benefits today. They were seen as great benefactors to British society and built, among other things, the Tate Gallery in London.

The building of Europe and America's great cities

The prosperity that marked this time is evident in the towns and cities of Europe and America. Their ornate buildings and institutions were built to impress. They became more and more grandiose. By the mid-19th century they often looked like Greek temples which announced their glory and power, particularly in Britain. We still unthinkingly enjoy and live in these buildings, many of which are now our concert halls and museums and contain artefacts stolen or bought at exploitative prices from colonies. If museums in Britain and America gave back all these exhibits there would no doubt not be much left (Moses, 2017).

Later, at the beginning of the 20th century, America began to impress too. The Woolworth building, for example, looks like a great cathedral: a testament to the religion of capitalism. These buildings are, in themselves, a great resource. They still impress and announce a sense of superiority which is important in the lucrative tourist industry.

Many of the houses owned by the UK National Trust, a non-governmental organisation that owns many British historic houses, were built by slave owners or traders, and some were built with the very generous compensation money that was given to people who lost potential wealth because of the abolition of slavery. Andrew Hann, a senior historian at English Heritage said, when a database was published of those who were given compensation on the abolition of the slave trade:

> It shows that certainly some country houses were built and refurbished with the proceeds of slavery, and particularly of slave compensation, which provided a substantial influx of capital for landowners in that period. But these records are only the tip of the iceberg because you've got the ongoing benefits with the proceeds of slavery circulating in these country houses for centuries earlier. The database shows who had slave-related property at the time of emancipation. (Manning, 2013)

There is no suggestion, when one visits National Trust houses, that their properties do not thoroughly belong to Britain, though much of the ostentatious wealth was brought to the UK from exploited colonies which used the labour of slaves. The possessions that are found within them, including ivory, animal skins, hard woods, jewels, precious metals, china and beautifully crafted objects, are, in the main, bought exploitatively or stolen from British colonies.

The same is true of American gracious historic houses. I have myself visited such houses in Louisiana where slaves worked pitilessly to keep the house in order and facilitated a wealthy lifestyle for its owners. In one such house I asked about the slaves who worked there and was brushed off and ignored. Similar houses are to be found in the north of America, such the Royall House in Massachusetts.

Political and economic arrangements

White political and economic arrangements, sometimes called neoliberalism (Chomsky, 1999), have become globalised and are dominating the world stage, notwithstanding the pressure from Russia and China. In later chapters, I explore this in more detail as well as the present challenge to whiteness. This includes how China has decided to try to beat the West at its own game and organise its economy to make use of the capitalist systems while remaining communist in name. Although China's ruling party is very much in control, it has fostered entrepreneurialism, and living standards have greatly increased in recent years, rising from 1 per cent of global trade in 1978 to becoming a leading economy in 2013 (Luce, 2017). Along with greater wealth has come greater spending power, so consumerism is enthusiastically embraced and is now encouraged, a fact which western companies have lost no time in exploiting.

This entering of foreign markets by large global companies is happening throughout the globe. As a phenomenon, it is often called 'McDonaldisation', which is a way of saying that famous western brands like Gucci and Coca-Cola, as well as McDonald's, are sold worldwide, making global companies as rich as whole nations (Dearden, 2016:22). The first McDonald's restaurant was opened in China in 1990 and by 2008 there were 850. Other western fast food giants, such as Kentucky Fried Chicken, have a similar story (Menzies, 2016).

Russia is similar to China in some ways, though the economy is less controlled from the centre. When communism failed, state companies were privatised. In an apparent attempt to be fair, the population were given 'privatisation vouchers' (Klebnikov, 2002) which could be changed for shares. Most people did not understand how valuable these were and happily sold them for cash to people who knew how to exploit the situation – mostly those who worked in the industries concerned. A vast amount of money was made in this way and ordinary people have not shared in this wealth. Those who now run these industries and businesses have become what have been dubbed 'oligarchs' – fabulously rich individuals. Corruption followed as a dystopian mirror of capitalism (Pomerantsev, 2017).

So, although these countries are not ostensibly under the control of the

West, they have bought into a western way of 'growing' economies, thus contributing to the way that our growth economy is damaging the earth's ecology (Meadows, Randers, & Meadows, 2004) and perpetuating inequalities within society.

The supremacy of the English language

English (supremely the white language) has become internationally spoken so that most political negotiations and business arrangements worldwide are undertaken in English. This is even true within Europe. In the German company Deutsche Bank, English is spoken at work even when everyone present speaks German. In India and Africa, where there are many languages, English is used by people who do not have another that they share. It goes without saying everyone learns English. Foreign heads of government are sometimes translated on English-speaking news stations, but this is often unnecessary as they are able to speak in English well enough themselves without translation. Although the reason for this may be largely pragmatic, this fact subliminally gives English-speaking people the impression of dominance, even if this is not articulated consciously. It has had an insidious and colonising effect on other languages as is pointed out by English language teachers, Rapatahana and Bunce in their book *English Language as Hydra: It's impact on non-English Language Cultures* (2012). In their work, they noticed the way that the English language took control of learners. They said:

> Wherever [English] goes it takes with it, via its inherent discourses and structures – in a seemingly beneficial fashion – a whole panoply of inherent controls, expectations, attitudes and beliefs that are often counter to those of the learners themselves. (Rapatahana & Bunce, 2012:5)

Although English is not the most spoken language in the world – Chinese and Spanish come first – it is nonetheless very influential in that it is spoken in more countries than others (101 have English as a first or *de facto* language. Arabic is second, which is spoken in 59 countries). English equals Mandarin if you add together native and non-native speakers (1000 million).

Style of dress

White people's dress has become the dominant style worldwide. How people dress may seem superficial, but its visual impact has the psychological effect of dominating the world. Most business men and politicians wear the ubiquitous suit and tie. This is true even in the Middle East, where it is considered of utmost importance that the Islamic culture is not contaminated by western mores. Saudi Arabia provides an interesting exception to this rule.

A few years ago, when he was in South Africa, my husband, Peter Hawkins, visited Robben Island which was used to imprison black people in the apartheid era, including Nelson Mandela. Peter told me a very telling story, when describing this visit, which illustrates my point very nicely. Ex-prisoners of the island take groups round to show them what life had been like there. Peter's guide asked if an Englishman was present among the group he was showing round. When Peter acknowledged that he was, the guide, speaking to the group teasingly, suggested that, although Peter was wearing shorts and T-shirt, he was bound to have a tie in his pocket. He went on to say that one thing black people had learned from the English was, 'You'll never go to heaven when you die, unless you wear a collar and tie.' Then he mimed taking the part of the tie that hangs down and brought it up above his head as if to be hanged by it! A very succinct challenge to this dominant and dominating mode of clothing and one which challenged the way Britain had colonised, not only the country, but the culture.

White sport

Most of the sport played internationally is white – in fact, most but not all originated in Britain, including football, rugby, cricket, tennis, table tennis, hockey, gymnastics, golf, rounders, boxing, badminton and even baseball. Certainly, Britain colonised the world with sport. Non-white countries enthusiastically take part in these games, often outstripping the originators. Maybe this is an area in which previously colonised countries can get their own back! Nevertheless, sport gives the impression of the dominance of white – and particularly English – people.

When the British comedian, John Cleese, was interviewed on American television, he was asked to describe the difference between England and America. He said that one of them was that 'when we hold a world championship for a particular sport, we invite teams from other countries to play, as well'. This is a dig at the way that other countries do not play American sports a great deal, so that international matches are mostly internal affairs. Maybe this tells of Britain and America's different ways of becoming world powers!

Sport is often a multi-billion-dollar industry, and the controlling bodies of these extremely lucrative businesses are mostly controlled by white people. FIFA (Federation of International Football Association) made a lot of money for its bosses and is notoriously corrupt. Football is very popular worldwide and massive payments are made for television rights so, although black players are a core part of it and doing very well, Africa and other parts of the world pay huge sums to watch the games. In short, sport makes an enormous amount of money for white economies while other countries pay huge sums to watch.

Living with being white

In day-to-day life as a white person, most people do not think about their race or its privilege. Many protest that they are not racist and do not benefit by being white, if anyone suggests that they are, but they may not be taking into account the factors mentioned above which are just part of ordinary everyday life. It helps if you understand that racism isn't just a personal matter. There is:

- *personal racism*, which is about racist attitudes and actions in the present day
- *institutional racism*, which describes the way that organisations have entrenched racist assumptions within their systems
- *cultural racism*, which is embedded in the general culture and arises from deeply held assumptions that are rooted in the past.

Although we may not be as personally culpable for institutional and cultural racism, we do have responsibility to notice them and to work towards change.

As we have seen, we are still benefiting from the history of colonisation and slavery, and racist views are held in our culture and institutions.

Just as we benefit by past exploitation, we white people are also benefiting by present-day exploitation. Although we like to think that slavery is a thing of the past, there is a growing slave trade in today's world. Many people are trafficked all over the world, particularly to the West, and often used for sex or for domestic labour (Taplin, 2015). In addition to this, many people work as slaves or on starvation wages to ensure that the cost of our consumer goods is kept low. Evi Hartman (2016), a German researcher, found that, with a normal middle-class lifestyle in the West, you would have about 60 slaves working for you in sweat shops and elsewhere all over the world. She campaigns to put a stop to cheap goods bought on the backs of slave labour.

When McIntosh (1988) contemplated her privilege as a white person she clearly had all three types in mind as she thought of 46 ways that gave her privilege over black people. These are helpful in that they ground 'privilege' in everyday experiences that mostly go unnoticed. Although she wrote this list in 1988, her descriptions are still relevant today. Here are just two of them:

- I have no difficulty finding neighbourhoods where people approve of our household.
- Our children are given texts and classes which implicitly support our kind of family unit.

Many of the privileges are very subtle but nevertheless powerful. They are clear ways (often with subtleties embedded in them) in which white people are advantaged because of their race.

In the course of writing this chapter I have become very aware of the white privilege that I also take part in, every day of my life. So, following Mcintosh, what are some of the privileges that I avail myself of unthinkingly? Here are some:

- I can get a job as a psychotherapist without someone remarking on my colour and thinking that working cross-culturally is my natural place.
- I can collect my grandchildren from school without people staring at my clothes and the colour of my skin and without wondering where I come from.

- I can speak English and therefore make myself understood internationally without having to learn another language.
- I can see artefacts from around the world without having to leave my country.
- I can live my daily life without thinking that I might starve or be attacked so that my life is in danger.
- I can live in the country of my birth without feeling I should be asserting a different culture.
- I can meet someone I have previously contacted on email or the phone and they are not surprised by my colour when they see me.

Making such a list is a useful exercise for everyone to do so that their privilege comes home to them and is not just a theoretical construct. Readers might find it instructive to try this.

In this chapter, we have looked at the ways in which we benefit by being white, the unthinking ways in which we all participate in white privilege, even when we do not realise it. Unthinkingly partaking in white privilege is, itself, racist. However, racism is often thought of as more obviously prejudiced and more clearly motivated by categorising black people as 'other' and unbridgeably different. In recent decades, there have been various efforts to combat this kind of racism. In the next chapter, I will look at attempts that have been made to eradicate this. We will look at whether and how far this has been successful in eradicating racism of all types.

PART 2

....

THE EFFECTS OF
WHITE PRIVILEGE

....

CHAPTER 4

White Awareness Within a Culturally Diverse World

Introduction

Having established that white people *are* privileged, ways in which they are privileged and how this situation arose over the centuries, we now turn to how this privilege shows up in today's culturally diverse world. Though white people tend to be unaware of their own race within the modern world, their privilege and dominance are felt keenly by those who are not white. This is experienced as a particular form of prejudice we call racism. Racism is a form of prejudice which is experienced by a less powerful race, when they are abused or disadvantaged by a more powerful one (Bidol-Padva, 1972). We will see how that can be very overt or very subtle. The more subtle it is, the harder it is to challenge and rectify.

The very fact of there being 'races' is a subtle piece of racism. White people, through a sense of entitlement that is taken up as a natural right, invented the idea of race and then assumed themselves to be the top of the tree as the most capable, the most intelligent and even the most beautiful (Alcoff, 2015; Irvin Painter, 2010; Kendi, 2016). This situation has 'set in' as the norm so that white people now take their whiteness for granted – so much so that many white people do not normally see themselves as having a race at all (Dyer, 1997; Frankenberg, 1999; Ryde, 2009).

The most socially damaging outcome of white privilege is racism. However, it is easier for well-intentioned white people to see that racism is endemic in the country than to understand and experience white privilege as applying to themselves and their institutions. The often-used definition of racism is 'hatred of people of a different race'. However, the *Oxford English Dictionary's* definition is 'Prejudice, discrimination, or antagonism directed against someone of a different race, based on the belief that one's own race is superior.' This definition is still problematic as anyone may think their race is superior without that race being privileged. It is clearly different if a white person calls a black person a racist than if a white person calls a black person a racist as the issue of power is not acknowledged. We might say the black person is prejudiced or xenophobic, but not racist. Or we might think they have good reason to think in that way! An alternative definition is 'prejudice plus power'. This was first conceived by Patricia Bidol-Padva in her book *Developing New Perspectives on Race* – now out of print (Bidol-Padva, 1972).

In recent decades, there has been some attempt to tackle racist attitudes in white people and I will now explore how far this has been successful and whether or not the policies and practices for ensuring that racism is reduced are successful. If they are not, what prevents them from being so and what can be done instead? It seems to me that racism in white people will not really be challenged or changed until we are prepared to seriously take on board and understand the privilege we continue to benefit from and have enjoyed over the centuries.

Attempts to combat racism

Activists and politicians who are opposed to racism often try to eradicate it by simply insisting on non-racist language and behaviour – i.e. speaking and behaving in a politically correct manner. 'Politically correct' was first used as it is today in the 1980s but didn't become common practice until the 1990s when it was used to encourage people not to speak in a racist, sexist or prejudiced way against any minority group.

As I showed in Chapter 2, around that time there seemed to be a political will in a sufficient number of the population, and among politicians, to start to build a more equal, diverse and inclusive society. Although enough people accepted this idea for it to make political headway, it was by no means a universally espoused wish. However, the pressure to conform to this new consciousness was sufficient to bring about some changes in the UK, elsewhere in Europe and North America. Maybe this was because it was built on a sense that it was the moral thing to do. As I remember it, most people at that time would deny that they were racist and would try to ensure that they did not break the rules of political correctness.

Training courses for professionals such as social workers and the police were common and taught people how to avoid using racist language (Dominelli, 1988:61). From accounts given to me at the time, being shamed on these courses was a commonplace experience and many found them to be uncomfortable situations, to say the least. The anger of black people about the racism they experienced was understandably evident, both from black members of the training group and the trainers. The impression gained at the time, and by hearing people speak of it since, was that some white participants learned about their racism from these training sessions in a positive way. Others learned to hide their racist thoughts and feelings, privately saying they felt bullied and intimidated. Although those who led these courses may have felt that the people deserved the anger directed at them, on the whole, I think people learned to hide their racist views, even from themselves, rather than change them. The training therefore did little to change the attitudes of those people. They simply ensured that they did not espouse racist views at work and were very careful what they said to, and about, black people.

So how far has 'political correctness' been helpful in tackling racism? How successful has it been in helping white people to understand themselves and their privilege within a racialised society and a racist environment?

The combination of anti-racist laws and a societal attitude which makes racism something people do not like to admit to, is undeniably a great achievement. 'Political correctness' does, therefore, seem to have been at least partially successful, but I argue that insisting on anti-racist policies and practices is not sufficient in itself. Many social workers like Dominelli worked hard to try to get these policies in place (Dominelli, 2006a: 223). She writes of the need for good communication with all communities and the making of alliances with people of good will to achieve changes in both professional and public understanding of the needs of all communities. Her argument is that, if endorsed by local and national government, good communication can lead to lasting change (Dominelli, 2006b).

However, there were many attacks on those trying to bring anti-racist policies into practice by some politicians and professionals which 'peaked in 1993' (Dominelli, 2006b). At the time of the latest edition of Dominelli's book, anti-racist policies were still not satisfactorily in place. She points out that characterising the challenge to racism in social work as 'extreme political correctness', which she often heard said, was 'trivialising' the issues involved (2006b:223). Although Dominelli, and other great campaigners for social equality, worked hard to bring about a just civil society and to ensure that BME groups were treated fairly, there could also be a hardening of attitudes in some white people, groups and institutions, even when people appeared to be compliant with apparently new realities. At the time of writing this book, I would say that the laws of Britain, America and most European countries are not really the problem, as anti-discrimination laws are, on the whole, in place. More often, the problem is the, often private, attitudes of both the public and institutions, which still carry deeply held racist assumptions.

On the day that I write this, the coffee chain Starbucks has come under pressure to review its institutional racism after several racist incidents, the latest of which was when a black man was refused access to the restroom (toilet) although he was a paying customer, whereas a white man was allowed to use it, although he had not bought anything. The chief executive of Starbucks, who prides himself on the company's social responsibility, has initiated a campaign called 'Race Together' to combat racism in the organisation. He is even shutting about 8000 of his cafes for 'unconscious bias' training which will, of course, lose the corporation millions of dollars. He is reported to say that the training is 'designed to address implicit bias, promote conscious inclusion, prevent discrimination and ensure everyone inside a Starbucks store feels welcome'. On the face of it, this is admirable, but there is a degree of hypocrisy as loss of income from customers is, no doubt, a major reason for the speedy response. Liberal and socially minded policies are important markers of the Starbucks brand, but it is accused of doing nothing to address the fact that those at the top are mostly (but not all) 'pale and male' and they do not to address the way that poor black neighbourhoods are often 'gentrified' when a Starbucks store moves in. This is an example of the systemic nature of the difficulty we are facing. Seeing the problem as 'belonging' to individual staff members who will, properly trained, not act in racist ways, is not likely to be successful or persuade black people that they should not boycott the stores. In an apparent attempt to see the problem more systemically, Starbucks has encouraged staff to talk to customers about race so that an open dialogue can be initiated. While there may have been a genuine desire to address the stand-off between blacks and whites in Starbucks, it may not work in this form. The policy has been mocked on Twitter and the press as not a conversation people want to have over their lattes. Indeed, they do not.

Other groups within society which work to challenge racism include Kick it Out, which campaigns to put an end to racism in football, and SARI (Stand Against Racism and Inequality), which offers help and support to people who have suffered racist experiences and attacks. Other anti-racism campaigns and organisations have been successful at keeping a watchful eye on racism and calling people to task. Some governments have been more determined to stamp out racism and some less, but all have at least given lip service to disapproving of racism since anti-racist laws came on the statute book more than 50 years ago. As we will see, racism is nevertheless still with us today, despite it being illegal to discriminate against someone on grounds of race.

We now see many more black people on our screens than used to be the case, though they are still vastly under-represented. For instance, there is only a small number of black actors who receive an Oscar in spite of this being something of a *cause celebre*. Another example is the disproportionately large number of white MPs compared with black ones – a matter of shame for the political parties and other groups which profess to show that they are trying to do something to stamp out racism. Nevertheless, most British people would deny that they thought less of someone because of their race. This is an achievement in itself. Changing the rules and laws and insisting on equal opportunities does have some effect on the general attitudes of the population as a whole – but this is not the whole story.

Owning half-conscious assumptions, attitudes and prejudices

We seem now to have reached a place where no further improvement has been made for some time, and, in some cases, we seem to be returning to a time when racist attitudes were considered acceptable, particularly after the Brexit vote and the election of Donald Trump in America. So, should we try harder to implement present policies with more and more anti-racist campaigns and would this be successful in eliminating racism altogether?

I doubt it for four reasons:

- We are focusing on trying to give equality of opportunity to black people while not owning up to white privilege.
- We are saying that this is a problem for black people who need our help.
- Racist attitudes go underground because people privately have different attitudes to ones they acknowledge publicly.
- Racist attitudes are often unconscious so that even people concerned about these issues are not necessarily aware of their racism.

It is clearly difficult for white people to own how privileged they are. Most people do not think of themselves as being part of a powerful elite and the frustration of black people who experience this denial on a daily basis is palpable. I have spoken to many people who have one white and one black parent, for example, who are astounded at the difficulty that white people have in seeing that it is the white person, who has the problem rather than the black person. One such is Reni Eddo-Lodge, who has published a book called *Why I'm No Longer Talking to White People About Race*. She wrote: 'When I talk about racism, the response from white people is to shift the focus away from their complicity and on to a conversation about what it means to be black, and about "black identity"' (Eddo-Lodge, 2017).

She also says:

White privilege is the fact that if you're white, your race will almost certainly positively impact your life's trajectory in some way. And you probably won't even notice… Trying to convince stony faces of disbelief has never appealed to me, the idea of white privilege forces white people who aren't actively racist to confront their own complicity in its continuing existence. (Ibid.)

It is interesting to me that she gets 'stony faces'. I often get polite but slightly confused faces when I say that I am writing (again) about whiteness until

I save the day by saying that my interest is in diversity, thus not picking out anything specifically to do with whiteness. I do also sometimes get the response: 'That book is so needed', even by white people who are waking up to the realisation that it is white people who need to address the intractable issue of race today. In a group of white psychotherapists that I convened to help me with my doctorate research, one of the therapists said he couldn't understand how we could research this issue without black people being present. I had insisted that the group should just be for white people so that we were *not* reliant on black people to tell us about our whiteness. When the research finished, he sent me an email in which he said:

> Since the group disbanded, I have increasingly seen that my inability to elucidate on the experience of my own whiteness is itself a manifestation of a complacence so deep that I am only just recognising its existence. In a multiracial context, I suppose this sense of belonging to the group that has a confident certainty of its own acceptability is what I would bring, consciously or otherwise. This does not seem a particularly honorable or helpful legacy. (Mills, 2005)

We found that the very fact of focusing on whiteness made us more aware of the issues about its privilege, and more possible to see its impact on us. In my book, *Being White in the Helping Professions*, I wrote:

> Gradually, as I have started to look at it, whiteness has become less neutral and more figural for me. It is as if by staring at a blank page, I have begun to notice contours and shades that were not at first apparent. (Ryde, 2009:36)

This neutrality or invisibility – a sort of nothingness of whiteness (Aanerud, 1997; Dyer, 1997; Frankenberg, 1999) is one which is experienced by many white people including myself and people in my research group, as well as others I interviewed in the course of my research (Ryde, 2005). Although the idea that whiteness is invisible was dismissed by Alcoff (2015), who said that when she was growing up as white in the south of the USA she was only too aware of it, I am not convinced that this awareness of her whiteness was not because of her particular circumstances as she, while looking white, identifies as a Latino because this is her heritage. She cites white people's sense of superiority as evidence of their awareness so that: 'Whiteness…has been defined as having a selfhood as distinct from others – smarter, more culturally advanced, more typically rational, and thus naturally on top of the social pyramid' (Alcoff, 2015:86).

But my view is that white people do not usually go around thinking this consciously. It is just assumed in the background. It is likely to be denied if asked if this were the case. Its insidious, unconscious and denied nature makes it all the more powerful.

On the whole, white people are not aware of themselves as 'having' a race in the way they would be if the white race had been so named by black people and had been disadvantaged by this naming (Bonnett, 2000:120). Black people have not only been 'given' a race by white people but have then been examined and been the subject of research carried out by anthropologists and others to learn about their customs and cultures as a matter of interest in the same way as a botanist explores plants and a zoologist, animals.

Alcoff points out that for white people their whiteness is the 'cornerstone of their sense of who they are' (Alcoff, 2015:86). It shapes and defines their sense of identity. Questioning our whiteness is therefore not only giving up a privileged existence, it is giving up one's taken-for-granted identity – an identity based on entitlement within a racialised environment.

Carol Webber (2018), a white South African woman, who thought she understood racism and stood against it, was deeply shocked when a black presenter at a conference said 'never underestimate the desire of a black man to be white'. She went on to say:

> I have to say that I have thought about this statement over and over since the event and I have shared it with many people. I do think it has helped me to understand more about the depth of 'white privilege' that I have and the huge responsibility I have in using my skills, influence and relationships to try and better the lives of others that in many ways are less fortunate than myself. I do believe that many white people in South Africa are largely unaware of their 'white privilege' and the current response of white people to our employment equity practices [in recruitment and promotions] may also be seen as an indicator of this. (Webber, 2018)

This sudden shock on hearing how black men longed to be white is something I recognise from when my colleague said that she had 'no idea what a sense of self is'. Such experiences shake us out of our fixed worldview.

White people's feeling of unease in the presence of black people is probably because of an awareness that something is not understood about our privileged position. This is not always, or even often, conscious and might well be denied by most white people (Kincheloe & Steinberg, 1998:13). There are a good number who do understand *intellectually* that they are privileged in being white and even that they are still benefiting from colonisation and slavery in the past – though these may well just be people who have given the matter considerable thought – but do not know how to respond to this. In my research, I found numerous examples of people who did feel guilty about how they and other white people have treated and continue to treat black people (Ryde, 2009:76). Jacobs, a psychotherapist, noticed this sense of guilt and wrote:

> Probably better known to most of us than our race-based anxieties is our race-based guilt. Many of us feel guilty about the history of slavery and inequality that is so inherently contradictory to our democratic aspirations. The ugly and self-defeating combination of anxiety, guilt, shame and ignorance makes it all but impossible for even the most minor of cross-race interactions to proceed with the natural grace that is common in white-white interactions. (Jacobs, 2005:225)

However, the extent to which my interviewees and research partners felt guilty decreased the less personally responsible they felt for the racist past. It is harder for people to take on board that they might still benefit from past exploitation and that the attitudes of the past may still resonate in them today even if they do not consciously espouse them. It is a trickier problem than simply becoming aware of white privilege and changing our behaviour. I will explore this further and look at what might help in Chapter 8.

The new study of epigenetics (Gapp & Bohacek, 2017) is beginning to show that traumas experienced by an individual can be passed on to subsequent generations. Maybe the same can be said about prevailing attitudes such as white superiority. If this is 'hardwired' into white consciousness it is no wonder that it is hard to counter. This does not mean it cannot shift but it does mean that we have a hard struggle to generate fundamental change.

White people feeling under threat

In his book, *When China Rules the World*, Martin Jacques (2012) points out that China is set to take over hegemonic primacy from the West but is not understood as a threat to western domination by westerners, because the white neoliberal culture is so ubiquitous that another way seems unthinkable to them (Jacques, 2012:17). Jacques also points out that political leaders assume that China will fall in line with the West economically and accept western ways and the consensus of the 'international community' which is dominated by western cultural attitudes (Jacques, 2012:16).

There will be more about China in the next chapter, but I mention it here because the western response to the rise of China reveals the West's assumed ascendency of the neoliberal way. There will be more about neoliberalism in Chapter 10. Although politicians may view the rise of China and other nations strategically, it seems that some people have a more visceral response and feel under threat. For this reason, we are seeing a retrenchment to a past sense of 'home' and familiarity. This has become more obvious with the election of Donald Trump in America and the Brexit vote in the UK. Many people seem to be harking back to an earlier period when red-blooded patriotism was more readily expressed and accepted.

In 1961, Enoch Powell gave a speech on St George's Day in which he said that England (sic) herself should be untouched by the experience of empire so that returning 'empire builders' should find her basic, one-thousand-year-old nature unchanged. In stirring language, he said that those who knew England:

> would speak to us in our own English tongue, the tongue made for telling truth in, tuned already to songs that haunt the hearer like the sadness of spring. They would tell us of that marvellous land, so sweetly mixed of opposites in climate that all the seasons of the year appear there in their greatest perfection;

of the fields amid which they built their halls, their cottages, their churches, and where the same blackthorn showered its petals upon them as upon us; they would tell us, surely of the rivers, the hills and of the island coasts of England. (Powell, 1961)

When later, he saw the influx of black workers from the Caribbean and elsewhere, he was famously said to have predicted 'rivers of blood' to follow from it (Olusoga, 2016). The actual quote is, 'As I look ahead, I am filled with foreboding; like the Roman, I seem to see the River Tiber foaming with much blood.' His view of England was that it was essentially white and that any people who were apparently not white should be 'sent back' (Olusoga, 2016), a view which had not been expressed in recent decades but has more recently returned.

These opinions look old fashioned, but maybe they had only gone underground. If this is to really change, something more radical has to happen. Our cultural identities could be held more lightly and thus we could be more open to others. In that way, we could live more gracefully within our own culture and its assumptions and meet others in theirs' to forge a more peaceful world.

Having said that, it is also true that white people have an extra truth to take on board: their heritage of white supremacy, abuse of power and taking privilege for granted. This will have to be more deeply acknowledged, and let go of, if we are to live with integrity in any new dispensation. The fast-flowing stream of history is carrying us away from white supremacy as we will see in the next chapter, so we will certainly find that we cannot hold on to those privileges much longer. It is beholden on us to own our part in profiting from this exploitation.

No doubt the parlous state of the world with its conflicts and ecological degradation is not all the fault of white people, but it is my contention that it is right for us to take full responsibility for our major part in it. We white people have been particularly guilty of over-exploiting both other human beings and the natural resources of the world for our own benefit. We should not divert attention from that by blaming others or denying responsibility. Any extent to which others are to blame is for them to own up to. In later chapters, I will explore what this means for the future of white people and look in more detail at what we need to own and accept as ours.

CHAPTER 5

White Privilege Under Pressure

H aving explored how white privilege shows up in an increasingly complex world, we now turn to explore in more depth the ways that the West's neoliberalism has brought about a globalised world in which white privilege is under pressure. The world is changing dizzyingly fast and is also becoming more and more interlinked, though still culturally diverse. As I will show, pressure is exerted by both internal and external factors and the consequent systemic changes can lead to conflict as well as co-operation in this more apparently interconnected world. In this chapter, I will explore the effects of globalisation and the ways in which white dominance is being challenged.

Globalisation is a complex phenomenon including the interconnection of trade, the global traffic of powerful private capital and businesses, cultural exchange and influence and the ease of communication – particularly with the growth of the internet, cell phones and social media. However, as Menzies (2016) points out, many of the changes have led the world to appear more homogenous than it really is, such as showing similarities in dress and lifestyle. This could simply imply that a globally dominant culture is becoming more possible, but she points out that these changes are superficial and conflicts that arise over cultural difference and intolerance of difference remain.

> The theory of cultural convergence, although endorsed in popular discourse, is not supported by research. One can be relatively confident that for the conceivable future, cultural differences will persist and increasing integration will expose these differences to a much greater extent than ever before. (Menzies, 2016)

Menzies cites, for example, the culture in Singapore which is more 'relationship based', in contrast to America which is more 'transaction based'. Although both America and Singapore have flourishing 'modern economies' and may look superficially similar, their way of going about making business arrangements and contracts are quite different. These differences are not just based on established practice but on the underlying cultural values and assumptions which govern practice (Hawkins & Smith, 2006; Menzies, 2016). So, although in some ways it looks as if global cultures are converging, this may be an illusory perception, and there is some evidence that there is a retrenchment into asserting difference between one's own culture and that of others (Luce, 2017).

The apparent familiarity with other cultures that globalisation brings means that white dominance is revealed more clearly. It indicates that we are now experiencing a reaction to white dominance and privilege from non-white people, as can be seen, for instance, in the writing of Coates (2017), Kendi (2016), Eddo-Lodge (2017) and Olusoga (2016). At the same time, there is a backlash from white people to the greater prominence of black people who assert their equality, particularly with white people who are themselves disadvantaged in other ways (Alcoff, 2015:5; Eddo-Lodge, 2017). Understanding the needs of differently disadvantaged groups is always fraught and complex, since class, race, gender, sexuality and so on all interact and intersect with each other in complex ways – and trying to decide which is the worst disadvantage is a fruitless and destructive pursuit, as Collins and Hill point out in their book *Intersectionality*: 'The major axes of social divisions, for example race, class, gender, sexuality dis/ability and age operate not as discrete and mutually exclusive entities, but build on each other and work together' (Hill Collins & Bilge, 2016:vii).

Nevertheless, each group is also distinct with its own history and present-day trajectory, and those who are disadvantaged may well feel that other groups are being favoured. Refugees being given accommodation in an apparently unfair way is an example that causes great resentment. This dynamic follows an old familiar pattern. We saw the same thing in the past when waves of immigrants moved into deprived neighbourhoods and then progressed up to an area that was more 'desirable' as new immigrants arrived and took the less favourable housing – both groups competing with indigenous people for housing resources, whether these were acceptable to indigenous groups or not.

Some white liberals have recently reacted against the idea of white privilege within the politics of anti-racism. They maintain that what they call 'identity politics' is not helpful as it is divisive and fragmenting (Lilla, 2017). To me this is an untenable position. If little progress has been made towards community integration by learning to tolerate difference better, it does not help to ignore the differences in culture between diverse groups or assert that we should look beyond it, as Lilla does in his book, *The Once and Future Liberal* (Lilla, 2017). This is particularly true as one group – the white race – is privileged and still benefiting from past privilege. That is likely to be a running sore if it is not addressed. In fact, rather than the world being ready to move on from identity politics, this chapter shows how global attitudes have hardened in recent years and become more polarised, and how this divergence increasingly drives conflict and lack of understanding. We need to address this directly rather than naively assert that we are now able to see beyond our differences and live harmoniously.

Some people may think we are ready to progress because, as explored in Chapter 2, there are now anti-racist laws in place which should ensure that hate crimes are prosecuted in law. But hate crimes are still on the increase as we will see below. Although these laws have not been entirely successful in reducing hate crime, they do show that there is some intention to create a less discriminatory society following many campaigns to stamp out racism along with other types of hate crime such as those against gays. The fact that these laws are not truly successful demonstrates that they do not carry a sufficient number of the population with them. As we saw in the last chapter, white people who joined with non-whites in campaigning to put an end to racism must face their lack of overall success in spite of changes to the law. My contention is that this is at least partially because we, white people, of all persuasions, do not face up to our culpability and complicity in maintaining the unjust status quo. The era where white people could feel good about themselves merely because they advocate equal rights for all seems to provide a less plausible stance now. Whites can no longer leave their own liability unchallenged. We must acknowledge the way we are responsible for inequalities that still exist with their roots in our history and culture, as we saw in previous chapters.

In this context, the Swedish example is interesting. Hübinette and Lundström describe Sweden as a white nation in crisis (Hübinette &

Lundström, 2015). They show how the Swedish population had, in the past, considered Sweden to be a country which is 'pure' white. They had regarded their Nordic race as the elite of all white peoples. In 1968, there was a 'turning point' where Sweden became a more liberal country and, among many other liberal policies, espoused anti-racism (Hübinette & Lundström, 2011). They nevertheless saw themselves as *white* liberals so that anyone who was not white was automatically 'not Swedish'. Hübinette and Lundström describe a situation in which there is now mourning for the loss of 'white Sweden' as more and more non-whites have become Swedish, many of whom were born in Sweden to immigrant families and have permanently settled there. With the coming of more non-white immigrants, racism has become more evident and has led many Swedish people to mourn the loss of 'good Sweden'. Their self-image as one in which they are the world's leading liberal nation is challenged and they have now to take on board the fact that, when this paper was written in 2015, there were 40 seats taken by Sweden Democrats (SD) in the Riksdagen (Swedish parliament), which is just over 10 per cent of the total. (Their number is increasing and at the time of writing this chapter, it is 49.) SD is a far-right, anti-immigration party in parliament and seems to be threatening Sweden's liberal consensus. Besides the racism that is emerging in the present, it is evident in the country's history as well. Carl Linnaeus was the first person to create a 'race classification' in the mid-1700s and Anders Retzius invented the skull or cephalic index in the 1850s which became the principal method within the 'white' world for classifying race membership. As we saw in Chapter 2, this pseudo-scientific method was later used in America by the anthropologist Samuel George Morton. The Swedish Institute for Race Biology was founded in 1922 and a 'race hygiene' and eugenicist project was created at the same time. This was not dissolved until 1975.

Hübinette and Lundström show how Swedish people have now entered a new phase they call *Swedish Melancholy*, in which the mourning of the foundational idea of whiteness is challenged. They say that this period is:

> generally characterized by a neoliberal economy and a Neo-Conservative culture, by the dismantling of the welfare state and its replacement with a workfare regime, by colonial nostalgia, by the illiberal turn and Islamophobia, and by a general crisis mentality and feelings of fear and anxiety concerning

everything that is regarded as foreign, non-white and non-Christian. (Hübinette & Lundström, 2015:431)

In order to resolve this stage of 'melancholy', Hübinette and Lundström have this to say:

> In the future, it is our conviction that the disentanglement of Swedishness from whiteness is absolutely necessary in order to be able to deconstruct a Swedishness which does not allow non-white Swedes to be Swedish. This form of Swedishness also traps white Swedes in this melancholic state through the aporia-like double-edged images of the phantasms of 'old Sweden' and 'good Sweden', that is through the longing for and the mourning of the passing of both the first and the second phases of hegemonic whiteness in Sweden. Our hope for the future is therefore that a transformative moment will come true, open up and unlock this current regressive closure which we diagnose as 'white melancholia'. This will allow the necessary and definitive demise of both 'old Sweden' and 'good Sweden'. However, in order to be able to accomplish and reach this moment of transformation it is absolutely necessary to acknowledge the fact that the object of love is irretrievable and irrevocably lost forever, no matter how painful that may be to take in and accept. (Hübinette & Lundström, 2015:434)

It is my contention that, in order to be able to work through and let go of the mourning for their whiteness, they may also need to acknowledge the guilt and shame that comes with accepting the privilege and dominance which the old Sweden had and still has through unquestioningly identifying with being white. I discuss this more in Chapters 6 and 7.

As I was finishing the book, *Being White in the Helping Professions* (Ryde, 2009), Barack Obama became President of the United States of America. The thought crossed my mind at the time that the book might soon be out of date. If a black person could be voted into the most powerful position in the western world, was race becoming less of an issue? I soon realised that white hegemony was not in fact broken and it now looks like a very naive hope indeed. If white dominance had been dissolved, the colour of the president's skin would not have been of interest either positively or negatively. Coates, in his book, *Eight Years in Power: An American Tragedy* (2017), contends that Barack Obama managed to genuinely inhabit his blackness while also managing to communicate his 'affection for white America without fawning over it' (Coates, 2017:8) thus making himself into a possible president for all sections of the population. This herculean task of not buying into the usual splits that human beings make was an extraordinary achievement at this time in history. Those on the less powerful side of racism are not normally given real chances, even if an apparent nod is given to them. And it did not last. A backlash was inevitable. Coates points out that: 'Obama needed to be a Harvard-trained lawyer with a decade of political experience and an incredible gift for speaking to cross sections of the country; Donald Trump needs only money and white bluster' (2017:336).

So, what does it mean to be white in a post-Trump, post-Brexit, post-rise of European-right-wing-worldview – and how is it possible to make a positive contribution to this world that is becoming more connected and tolerant – and one where white domination is truly challenged? How can we ensure that we do not flip between a desire for tolerance and a backlash to apparently safe certainties? In the ebook, *The Brexit Crisis*, Laleh Khalili says, 'To counter such a bleak future, mass mobilization is necessary – and any form of progressive mass mobilization has to recognize that class politics are always articulated through a politics of race' (2016:2).

I agree that there could well be a bleak future, and something needs to be done, but I am not at all convinced, by past experience, that 'mass mobilization' is likely to be successful if it progresses by appealing to reason, righteous anger and proceeds through political lobbying. Although this may have some short-term success, it is likely to add to polarisation. Any apparent victory may well cause a swing in the other direction. At the end of this chapter, and later in the book, I will explore a different approach to the necessary change, but first I look at the different ways in which the pendulum swings, starting with global threats.

Global threats

Many authors have suggested that we are seeing unprecedented improvements in the living conditions of people worldwide – through a reduction in wars, disease and famine (Harari, 2015). Notwithstanding the partial truth of this, the number of very serious threats globally have vastly increased. There has been a huge explosion in the population, which is set to increase exponentially. When I was born, the world population was around two billion. It is now, over 70 years later, more than seven and a half billion. At the same time, climate change is starting to have a devastating effect on the world. There are many signs of this change, including a huge decrease in insect populations, needed for pollinating food crops and, while there are droughts in certain areas globally, there are floods elsewhere. Huge populations tend to mean a greater exploitation of the earth's resources and an increase in carbon found in the atmosphere, with an accompanying rise in temperatures. Providing populations with enough food and water is becoming increasingly difficult and we are likely to see growing numbers of 'economic' migrants moving to 'more fortunate' countries.

Already there is a massive crisis related to the number of displaced people worldwide, not only because of conflict within and between nations but also through degraded environmental conditions. Pope Francis speaks of this in his ground-breaking encyclical *Laudato Si: On Care for Our Common Home*. He says:

> There has been a tragic rise in the number of migrants seeking to flee from the growing poverty caused by environmental degradation. They are not recognized by international conventions as refugees; they bear the loss of the lives they have left behind, without enjoying any legal protection whatsoever. Sadly, there is widespread indifference to such suffering, which is even now taking place throughout our world. Our lack of response to these tragedies involving our brothers and sisters points to the loss of that sense of responsibility for our fellow men and women upon which all civil society is founded. (Francis, 2015)

This clearly shows that 'economic migrants' are not a separate phenomenon from refugees who are fleeing conflict. We are one world, and all are responsible for the suffering found in it.

What we are seeing is a global crisis on many levels and in many ways, with populations taking up more and more polarised positions in relation to these threats. The cultural divide between western nations and other parts of the world (as well as non-white people who live within western nations) is, at the same time, centuries old but also newly minted in the polarising world of today.

In spite of voting for a black president it has become all too clear that a wholesale change in consciousness towards racial equality in America has not happened. In fact, the vote for Donald Trump as president represents a huge backlash, as is pointed out by Ta-Nehisi Coates (2017). Nell Irvin Painter suggested that Donald Trump's cry to 'make America great again' probably means 'make America white again' (Irvin Painter, 2016).

In the UK, there is a similar dynamic active in those who voted for Brexit on the grounds of wishing to 'secure the borders' (Emejulu, 2016:ch 7). Since the referendum, it has become clear that many people within the country are hostile to foreigners (Akala, 2016; Eddo-Lodge, 2017; Emejulu, 2016). The rhetoric of the campaign, particularly from the UK Independence Party, has encouraged people to own their dislike of foreigners. The cry is to 'control our own borders' and this clearly sends a signal to politicians to limit the number of immigrants of any sort from entering the UK. There is a sense that other white people – i.e. western European in origin – were not meant to be included in this. In an echo of the hostility to eastern Europeans in 18th-century America, the clamour to leave the European Union greatly increased when the EU expanded to include eastern European countries such as Romania and Poland. Information showing how immigrants are net contributors to GDP (gross domestic product) and provide irreplaceable staffing in our public services, seems to make no impression on general attitudes. Racist hate crimes have soared since that time and headlines in some newspapers have become more openly racist. According to government figures, the number of race hate crimes in the UK during 2016/17 was 62,685 whereas it was much lower in 2015/16 at 49,414 – a 26 per cent rise. In 2014/15, the number was 42,430 which represents a rise of 47 per cent since then (Gov.UK, 2016–17). There was a significant rise year on year during that time.

Immediately following the Brexit vote, a series of chapters were written in an ebook, *The Brexit Crisis*. One of the authors, Akwugo Emejulu, clearly expresses her anger at the various narratives about whiteness emerging from and surrounding the result of the vote. This included the way that it was assumed that white, working-class people felt themselves to be victims of immigration and that other white people were (maybe smugly?) appalled at the increase in violence against foreigners. She felt that their dismay was surreptitiously appealing to black people to exculpate them:

> Finally, whiteness cloaks itself in innocence by arriving late to scene and adopting an identity of 'ally'. I question those who now claim to stand shoulder to shoulder with me when they also maintain, without irony, that a focus on race and 'identity politics' fractures the left at a time of crisis and undermines class politics. I question those who now only seem to care about racism and xenophobia when Brexit has used their bodies as borders. I question those who now believe racism is real because they have witnessed it with their own eyes. I also question those who seek to extract from me and other people of colour our emotional labour to absolve them of responsibility.
>
> I am not looking for allies; I want collective action. We face an uncertain future. Let us be honest about our past and our present if we truly seek to dismantle white supremacy. (Emejulu, 2016:2)

These words offer a prescient challenge to white people and we should listen to it.

The rise of China on the world stage

The threat to white supremacy and privilege from non-white people within European borders does seem to be increasing, but our privileged position is threatened internationally as well. In his book, *When China Rules the World*, Martin Jacques (2012) argues that (or, maybe, shows how) China's rise to power is inescapable and it is becoming ever clearer that it has a self-confidence based on its sense of itself as an ancient civilisation rather than a nation, and having a history of achievement that outshines Europe's. It is only fairly recently that it has become more widely known that China 'discovered' America and Australia in the 14th century before Europeans did (Menzies, 2016). Of course, they did not really discover them as they were already known to the people who lived there! However, it has certainly been taught to westerners that Europeans 'discovered' these parts of the world, and

China having been there first was apparently not known. I discussed this with a Chinese friend who was amazed herself to discover this. Many important scientific and technological inventions were made by Chinese people well before Europe discovered or invented them, such as paper making, movable type printing, gunpowder, compasses, alcohol, the mechanical clock, tea and silk production. Certainly, until 1400, China was vastly more technologically advanced than Europe (Diamond, 2013).

Following China's great voyages which led to discovering new lands, it did not try to dominate the world, as Europe did, but closed its borders and even expunged evidence of these discoveries from the record both internally and externally (Menzies, 2016), thus shutting the rest of the world out. This situation continued into the 20th century when, after much conflict and the involvement of the Soviet Union, a communist government was formed. It thus established a different style of government to capitalism's economic arrangements and western-style democracy. In spite of ostensibly advocating equality, China remained a relatively poor country with only an elite having wealth. However, the current President, Xi Jinping, now seems to have decided to beat the west at its own game by encouraging what has been called 'state capitalism'. In 2013, Xi Jinping announced that 'market forces rather than the State would now play a decisive role in the Chinese economy' (Kurlantzick, 2016:1). In recent years, China has had stunning economic growth and its huge population seems to make its rise as the next superpower unstoppable. In the meantime, the US's economy is less dominant on the world stage and it has seemingly over-reached itself by trying to impose its ascendancy on countries which threaten it, making it less popular with other nations that have not 'bought into' it's cultural pre-eminence. Western countries, and particularly America, seem to feel that countries who do not espouse their values and political arrangements are, by definition, at best wrong-headed and at worst 'rogue states'.

Jacques contends (2012) that white, western nations have been predominant for so long that it is hard for them to see any other way of being successful or that other cultures may have legitimacy. He says, 'We have come to take Western hegemony for granted. It is so deeply rooted, so ubiquitous, that we think of it as somehow natural' (Jacques, 2012:53).

America took over from the British Empire as the global power and the fact that both were of European stock and shared, more or less, the same culture and language meant that this takeover happened without major upset (Harari, 2015). Britain is still acknowledged as having a 'special relationship' with America and has tended to stand 'shoulder to shoulder' with her in conflicts. White western European hegemony has therefore been continuous for almost 300 years.

While it has been so solid as a world power and without rivals, the western world has felt secure, like a lion that can afford to go to sleep and will wake and cuff someone who has got out of line. Now, with the Islamic and Chinese (and Indian) challenge to this cultural supremacy, we are seeing a more aggressive stance to this assumption. Jacques (2012) shows how American, and other western nations' idea of modernity is no longer the only valid one and, under this pressure, other ideas are seen as a threat (Jacques, 2012:15). Trump's retrenchment to 'America first' might well illustrate just this.

The challenge from the Islamic world

Important as the challenge from China is, the challenge from Islam may be more urgent, especially as it has the most coherent cultural critique of our western world. This entails a critique of white hegemony generally. This critical evaluation of the West is not, or even mostly, held by extremist and violent groups within the Islamic world such as ISIS, the Taliban and Boko Haram. Islamic culture entails a much more widespread critical view of the worst excesses of western materialism. According to this Islamic perspective, the historical developments in the West since the Enlightenment in the 18th century, when individualism and rationalism became important ideas, have led to an over-individualist philosophy, resulting in modern times in *laissez-faire* attitudes to sex and other behaviours that Islam considers immoral. This critique extends to irresponsible social norms and leads to inadequate care for elderly and other vulnerable people (Shari'ati, 1980). This point of view is shared by many African people and those from other non-western cultures (Lago, 2011).

In recent years, Muslims have become more assertive in expressing their difference as a community and have taken pride in their culture. Hostility to Muslims has grown to the extent that it has become known as Islamophobia.

Some young Muslims are so enraged by the treatment of their religion and culture that they join the global fight or 'jihad' – while other Muslims deplore this, pointing out that Islam is a peaceful religion. This situation is a violent running sore within global societies and the polarisation between the two is not conducive to resolution. We have here a cultural clash which seems irreconcilable and it obviously is not just a simple matter of different cultural norms. The white side is culturally dominant and the privilege which comes with that gives the clash a potency that would not otherwise be present (McIntosh, 1988).

It seems likely that the days of white dominance are numbered. I notice that the term 'post-western' has entered the language. What, if anything, might bring an end to white privilege and these cultural polarisations? It could be based on:

- *economic developments* as non-white nations, such as China, become richer and therefore more influential
- *cultural difference* from cultures that are not prepared to put up with white dominance any more
- or, most likely, a mixture of both.

President Putin in Russia has suggested that there should be several 'axes of power' in a 'polycentric world' (Luce, 2017). This contrasts sharply with America's insistence that peace is only possible if countries adopt western-style democracy. To those in the West, Putin's idea seems to give licence to countries in which human rights abuses are rife. However, western nations merely asserting that western-style democracy is the only peaceful way forward for the world is clearly problematic. Western nations are not blameless when it comes to creating conflict or in ensuring the rights of minorities. Cavanaugh points out that the liberal nation state prides itself on its rational decision making when going to war but says that they 'regrettably find [themselves] obliged to bomb [Muslim states] into liberal democracy' (Cavanaugh, 2009)! In addition, short-term thinking is almost inevitable in parliamentary democracies, borne of the necessity to keep electorates on side. Frequent elections can mean that policies which aim to improve important matters such as climate change might be overturned at the next election.

In later chapters, I explore how promoting dialogue about knotty issues may be more productive (see Chapter 8).

Addressing the fault lines

There are many fault lines in cultural and racial difference which cause tension (including those from black and other non-white people who live within western countries). These fault lines are caused by underlying cultural differences and the way in which we human beings tend to only have empathy for 'people like us' (Bloom, 2018:7). In the next chapter, I will explore how I understand the cultural difference between white western and many other global cultures by examining their underlying and more fundamental mores, including the difference between individualistic and collectivistic cultures.

At present, there is a tendency towards a polarising split between western countries that are relatively peaceful and wealthy and non-western countries, many, though not all, of which are impoverished and riven with conflict. When the white, western world looks towards non-western countries, it tends to see countries where individual human rights are not respected, and which are riven by power struggles. It sees nations where the ones who 'win' are likely not to be pro-western, are incompetent in their administration of government and often corrupt. Non-western countries look to the West and see an arrogant belief in their customs being the best and the only legitimate ones, a culture in which grossly immoral behaviour is tolerated and one that exploits other countries for their own gain while denying that this is so.

What can be genuinely helpful in the light of this chasm of difference, which is potentially a profound turn in the political and social landscape? My view is that we need an attitude that attempts to find compassion for all individuals and groups in society and to understand what it is to walk in their shoes. Deep understanding is what underlies all reconciliation as well as psychological healing (Orange, 1997) and finding this understanding is a journey that requires us to:

- listen at every level to all within the human family and the world in general

- show humility in the face of differences
- have the courage to show up in the front line to confront society's ills.

These are big demands, but we live in times that require more of us than ever before. We need people who can facilitate dialogue between cultures with the help of more recent approaches and theories that find ways to contain and fruitfully work with the ubiquitous polarities we generate regarding the cultural clashes I have outlined. We are bound to stumble and struggle but with mutual support, maybe we can make a significant contribution to present ills and slowly build up numbers of people who not only comprehend other people's views, *but understand their own complicity and culpability* and are prepared to take responsibility for it and do something about it. Maybe Starbucks (see Chapter 4) would have been more successful in persuading people of its genuine anti-racist intentions if it acknowledged white blameworthiness in racial tensions. This I will explore in more detail in future chapters.

But first I will explore how the world can look very different from other cultural perspectives. Besides white people needing to understand and accept their privilege, they must also understand that their way of seeing the world is not shared by all and it is to this that I turn in the next chapter.

CHAPTER 6

Features of Cultural Differences

Having explored the way that the white, western, privileged nations have been most instrumental in bringing about a globalised world, we can see how this has led to whiteness itself being under pressure. We now turn to look in more detail at differences in culture and how these play into present global tensions. As I have shown, dominance and privilege are so unquestioningly built into white, western culture that it becomes taken for granted, appearing 'natural'. White people are so embedded in this culture, and it is so apparently normal, that often we do not thoroughly understand how our own culture fits into a world of different cultures. This chapter will explore in more detail the ways in which cultures can vary. These differences in constructing our respective worlds have led to serious misunderstandings in the west by white people. There will be a particular focus on the difference between individualistic and collectivist cultures.

There are many similarities in the human experience whatever culture we come from – we all live with the knowledge that we will suffer illness and die and so will our loved ones. We are all subject to the needs of the body for sustenance, warmth and sex, and we are all attached and bonded to our families who are important for our well-being. This means that we are capable of understanding and empathising with other humans when they suffer, notwithstanding a tendency to empathise more with our own family and community (Bloom, 2018). However, there are many dissimilarities in values, norms and assumptions between cultures and this leads to different ways of behaving and living. This is evident to anyone who strays from their own culture and does not live within their own 'bubble'.

Many authors have tried to categorise these differences in order to try to understand them and to help people navigate their way through this terrain. (Hofstede, 1980; Kluckhohn & Strodtbeck, 1961; Sue & Sue, 1990) They attempt to show how different cultures have different ways of seeing and understanding the world. These authors often use different categories of human experience such as 'power distance', which shows how power is distributed within the culture, and 'uncertainty avoidance index', where those with a high uncertainly avoidance have very clear codes of behaviour and are not able tolerate uncertainty (Hofstede, 1980). Many of the different dimensions of culture are the same or similar to those in each of the authors' taxonomies, but it is also striking that there are many differences as well, so none can be said to be exhaustive and there are probably many more than have been suggested by these authors. Hofestede, Kluckholn and Stodtbeck are all American, as are Derald and David Sue, although they are also of Chinese heritage. The dimensions they have categorised are therefore not 'culture free' themselves, as none of us can understand the world without seeing it from our own perspective (Reason & Bradbury, 2001:4).

In saying that these categories are not in themselves culture free, it is also evident that they are using a white lens on cultural difference. Although Sue and Sue are of Chinese heritage, they are also schooled in American culture. Furthermore, these kinds of categories are in danger of stereotyping people according to their cultural membership. They could therefore encourage us not to see the complexities and variants which are due to differences in experiences arising from time to time in the lives of individuals. For instance, in an interaction with someone from a different culture who seems to be deferring to me, I could have this question in mind: 'Why is this person unnecessarily deferring to me?' rather than the more useful one: 'Could my difficulty in understanding this person be because of difference in culture?' If I take into account Hofstede's cultural dimensions, the thought could then be: 'If he is seeing "power difference" in a way that is not usual for me, it may explain the way he is deferring to me.' I can then approach the contact with this person with that tentatively, rather than definitely, in mind.

Here is an example from my work (which is in the UK). I have a psychotherapy client who had to go to the Job Centre (people are required by law to attend the Job Centre in the UK if they are unemployed and want to receive benefits). The official there asked her what her doctor had said about how long it would take for her foot to heal. She was puzzled and dismayed by this question and asked me how she could be expected to know the answer. I could see that she was genuinely shocked to have been asked this question and I guessed that she had different cultural norms concerning interactions with doctors. I explained that in England it was usual and even encouraged to ask a doctor about your medical condition, but my client said she could not bring herself to ask as it felt so rude. She also felt it was unacceptable to explain this to the Job Centre official. Neither the doctor nor the Job Centre official understood that there was a difficult cultural issue in my client's problem with this. In thinking about this dilemma with my client, I did not immediately assume that this was a 'power distance' issue. However, the fact that I knew of Hofstede's categories alerted me to this possibility and I understood that my client's responses need not be a matter of her personality or mental health pathology. I was aware that she used to have a similar dilemma in speaking to me, but we had a well-established relationship and she had grown accustomed to treat me more like a family member that she could confide in. I asked my client what going to the doctors was like in the country of her birth. She told me that doctors were revered and asking questions was frowned on. With the client's permission, I explained this dilemma to the official at the Job Centre. She was very understanding and it helped them to communicate more effectively in the future.

A cultural map

In my research and later in my book, *Being White in the Helping Professions* (Ryde, 2009), I developed and explored two different cultural dimensions that seemed to me to be particularly useful for psychotherapists but also more widely applicable:

- emotional expression and emotional restraint
- privileging the individual and privileging the group.

Emotional expression is valued in psychotherapy, so it is important to recognise that if a client is reticent in expressing emotion, it is not necessarily pathological. Similarly, psychotherapists tend to focus on their client's individual needs and direction in life, which can seem very selfish to people who value the group (family and community) over the individual.

The two factors I chose can be expressed as polarities that I used to form a quadrant diagram on which cultures may be plotted as in Figure 6.1 below:

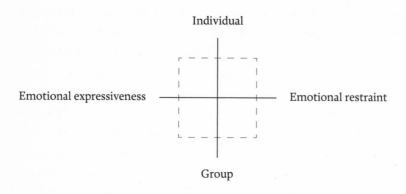

Figure 6.1: Culture quadrant diagram

It is problematic to place a culture on the diagram in a definitive way, as culture is not immutable and there are variations within any culture, but it gives us a useful indication. For instance, American culture tends to value the individual over the group, and emotional expression over restraint but there are sub-groups within American society that are different from this. The Amish are an example as they live much more communally than is usual in America (Corry, 2011). We can also use the map to place ourselves within the different cultures we are part of. Placing ourselves (rather than only doing so for others) helps us to experience the fact that we also live within a culture. Given that we all live in multiple cultures, we can do this for all the different cultures we live within.

For instance, we might find that our family culture, where a lot of emotion is expressed, differs in this regard from our work culture, where we might have to mask our emotions. We can therefore put ourselves in different positions depending on the different cultures we are part of. While the diagram does not cover all possible cultural differences, it does help us to easily orientate ourselves to two important variables and think in a more nuanced and culturally sensitive way where differences are not absolute but shade into each other.

Those from second or third generation immigrant backgrounds might find this particularly useful as they often have to struggle with apparently sharp differences between cultures at home and the culture of the society in which they live. It is easy to think that our own experience is just the natural and normal way, so it is helpful, as we live in a world of different cultures, to place ourselves on this diagram and try to understand our own cultural positions.

The difference between privileging the group or the individual in the diagram puts the two factors on a spectrum which can be useful in understanding such differences in a nuanced way. However, this difference is also described as two different types of culture: 'individualistic' and 'collectivist' (Triandis, 1995). This difference was pointed out to me by an Indian colleague who recommended a book, written by a fellow Indian, which showed me the importance of describing cultures in this way, in spite of the problem of over-simplifying the matter, as there are some fundamental differences that are hard to reconcile (Laungani, 2004). I am now of the view that a failure to understand the difference between these two can lead to serious difficulty when relating between cultures worldwide, a lack of understanding which results in many of the global tensions and conflicts we currently find being played out across the world.

In the white, western world, individualism is prevalent to one degree or another and the values inherent in individualism tend to be privileged in powerful western cultures. As we saw in the cultural quadrant diagram above, we cannot be hard and fast about this as individualism and collectivism can run along a spectrum and, as Triandis (1995:87) points out, certain situations, like being in church, can bring out more collectivist and less individualistic behaviours and vice versa. The collectivist culture of armies, including those of the West, is another example. The difference between emotional expression and restraint tends to cut across the divide between western and non-western countries. On the whole, more northern European cultures tend to be more emotionally restrained than those of southern Europe. As the difference in emotional expressiveness tends to cut across western and non-western countries, but individualism tends to be more western and collectivism more non-western, I am concentrating on that difference here.

Individualism and collectivism

In the last chapter, we saw how one of the ways that we, as white people, express our privilege is to take for granted that our values and norms are the right ones. In a general way, those from the white western world believe in the rights of the individual over the rights of the group, thus making us individualistic rather than collectivist (D'Ardenne & Mantani, 1999; Laungani, 2004; Triandis, 1995) in our cultural attitudes. As always, the situation is more nuanced than that statement implies as some of the subcultures within western society are more individualistic than others. Arguably, working-class culture can be more collectivist than middle-class culture (Savage, 2015). Mediterranean cultures tend to be more collectivist than more northern European countries. Being thoroughly embedded within the family and community in Italy and Spain, for instance, is an important part of the culture. However, as we saw in earlier chapters, these countries have not always been regarded as so thoroughly white as more northern European countries (Irvin Painter, 2010). In a conversation between Carlyle and Ralph Waldo Emerson, these two highly eminent and still admired men, called the French 'ape like' (Irvin Painter, 2010), for example. As we saw in Chapter 2, Emerson described real Americans (mostly from New England) as 'double distilled Englishmen' (Irvin Painter, 2010) and thought that immigration to the USA should be restricted to 'Anglo Saxons'. We also saw in the last chapter that there has been a Swedish opinion that they, as 'Nordic', are superior to other white peoples (Hübinette & Lundström, 2015).

On the other side, some non-western countries, under the influence of the western world, have developed individualistic characteristics within their cultural practices. For example, the leaders of some countries have tried to 'modernise', in other words 'westernise' themselves, such as Turkey when Atatürk was in power and Iran before the last Shah was deposed. This included the wearing of western clothes, encouraging western music, films and television and open displays of affection between the sexes. More recently, we have seen a backlash from the population and leaders alike, wanting to assert more traditional values.

While bearing in mind that differences can be more nuanced, here is a table that sets out to illustrate the differences between individualistic and collectivist cultures, and some of the differences in values and assumptions between them.

Table 6.1: Values and assumptions of individualistic and collectivist cultures

Values and assumptions	Individualistic cultures	Collectivist cultures
The unit of society is	The individual	The family or community
Individuals	Should develop their individual talents and abilities as far as they can	Should work towards the good of their family or community
The self	Is something that 'belongs' to an individual	Cannot be extricated from a group identity
Authenticity is	Important as we have a 'true' self and it is important to be true to it	About honouring the collective context and your role within it
Membership of community	Is there to support individual well-being	Is there to support the well-being of the community

If you look at the two columns you can see, for example, that the unit of society for collectivist cultures is not the individual but the family or community. In the same way, the 'self' is not something that 'belongs' to individuals. It cannot be extracted from a group identity. This different idea of the nature of the 'self' first came home to me when I was told by the same Indian colleague I mentioned above that when she first heard the term 'sense of self', she had no idea what it meant. To me it was a self-explanatory phrase – the use of the word 'self' here helps to make the point!

Another shock to my understanding of 'reality' came on reading *The Songlines* by Bruce Chatwin (1987) where he said that Aboriginals find their way through the landscape following the song of the path. They are part, not only of their community and family but the whole landscape and the creatures and plants found there. What I came to realise is that others experience life differently, and sometimes very differently, to the way I experience it.

These different ways of seeing and experiencing the world have their own internal logic and their own strengths and 'shadow' sides. The West tends to give great value, at least in theory, to protecting the rights of individuals. This includes an independent judiciary, freedom of the press and, at least in theory, protection of minority groups. But, at their worst, western nations tend to breed narcissistic individuals, bent only on their own desires, ignoring the needs of others, such as elderly parents, and pursuing a life of addictions to short-term pleasures, exploiting others rather than leading a life of service. As de Graaf, Wann & Naylor say in their book, *Affluenza*, in the West we have become addicted to short-term pleasures that the planet cannot afford to sustain (de Graaf *et al.* 2014). The apparently democratic political system often serves the purposes of powerful and wealthy interest groups, a situation that is mostly hidden and denied. White nations frequently lack empathy towards non-white people who suffer from war, famine and oppression, without taking into account that white, western people have been, and still are, complicit in what lies behind such conflicts and poverty.

We know about these conflicts as we see them daily on our screens, but it does little to encourage what Hawkins calls a 'wide-angled empathy' (2018, in press). Developing an ability to experience this type of empathy means feeling empathetic to all in any situation – seeing the world from all points of view. Wide-angled empathy therefore includes all nations and cultures. Our lack of this kind of empathy accounts for the fact that we are more horrified by a few people killed on streets near where we live than thousands killed far away. This may be 'natural' (Hellinger & Hovel, 1999) as our empathy instinctively flows to our 'kith and kin', but if we are to survive as a species in this globally connected world, we need to embrace all as our kith and kin – all those who share the planet with us, including the 'more than human' world (Abram, 1996). As Nora Bateson (2017) says:

Most of what matters now won't matter later. Coming generations will shake their heads at the sacrifices their ancestors made for material wealth. They will not care how much prestige you gathered, how many bitcoins you bought, who considered you famous, or even what widget or vaccination you invented. If humanity makes it to the next level in the evolutionary game, it will be through recognition of our interdependency to each other and to the organisms of our biosphere.

People who live within collectivist cultures may have a tendency to more easily empathise with kith and kin. However, compared with members of individualistic cultures, they give greater value to service of the family and the wider community, emphasising the importance of unselfish behaviour, including the value of hospitality to strangers (Lago, 2011). In collectivist cultures, correct ways of behaving are often prescribed by custom, so how individuals tend to fit into their family and community is a given. From a white perspective, their apparent lack of consideration of the rights of the individual can lead to certain groups and individuals being oppressed and their rights forfeited. At its most extreme, we see forced marriage imposed by threat of death, female genital mutilation and harsh punishments to dissidents, including those who do not conform to societal norms, such as homosexuals.

The dichotomy between individualism and collectivism is not a new phenomenon, though it has sharpened in recent decades. Even in Shakespeare's day, the clash between the values held in different positions produced high drama. Romeo and Juliet, for instance, asserted their individual rights for personal happiness with their own choice of partner. The audience, certainly nowadays, is on the side of the lovers and we assume Shakespeare was too. But the drama ends in tragedy, maybe underscoring the moral that it doesn't pay to go against the family. It could be that the audience in Shakespeare's day would have seen the story very differently and understood the position of the families more sympathetically. Shakespeare's genius consisted in allowing the tale to resonate with humanity generally, whatever their cultural position.

In the West, we tend to take for granted that those who have different cultural values to ours are 'backward', not as 'advanced' as we are, as if there was an inevitable process of development towards western ways. This idea is given credence because western culture tended to be more collectivist in the past, when extended families and communities were closer to each other than they are today. This, in itself, does not logically mean that the West is more 'advanced'. In fact, we are now seeing that many of the changes in western culture have in recent decades led to rampant consumerism with attendant ecological disaster – an escalation of mental health problems and greater physical ill health caused by unhealthy lifestyles. This does not mean that everything about the western world is rotten, but it does call into question the idea of continuous upward progress and superiority to non-western ways.

As I am a psychotherapist working with asylum seekers and refugees, I am in a position to talk to people who come from collectivist cultures (in Africa and the Middle East, for example) and now live in Britain's more individualistic world. My clients are usually particularly critical of the licence given to young people to develop their individuality, unsupervised by their family. They see young people dressing in a sexually provocative way, allowed to go out at night and mix with the opposite sex – even having complete sexual freedom. These young people are seen to have their own life with their peers and to feel little duty to take part in family life. They see old people living in 'homes' away from anyone who loves them or on their own where they may be lonely and neglected, rather than in the family. To them, British culture looks selfish and callous. They are concerned about their own children picking up western ways and are very perturbed when their adolescent children start to rebel and want the freedoms that are taken for granted by their white school friends. I have pointed out to my clients that in western culture it is quite normal for teenagers to be difficult and rebellious. One of my clients did not know what to make of it when her children refused to help in the house. In her culture, this behaviour would have been completely unknown, and no one would have needed to insist on it. Children having a role in the family economy and day-to-day welfare is so much part of the culture that it would be unthinkable not to take part. Having adolescent children in the West is, for them, like a crash course in individualism. I do not see my job as being to change my clients' cultural perspective, but I do explain the puzzling and disturbing behaviour they encounter and help them to think through how they will respond to it.

Much of the anguish felt by non-white refugees is in relation to their families and communities, particularly as the parting from them has meant that traditional duties and customs cannot be properly carried out. An eldest son, for instance, cannot care for his parents and ensure the successful economy of the family. The anguish of a young man who is unable to meet these obligations far outstrips that which a westerner would feel by not being able to carry out family duties. This goes over and above missing those for whom there are attachment bonds, though that is felt very keenly as well, of course.

Now that we live in a globalised world, how can we respond to the tensions and conflicts that arise between cultures, particularly in the face of the dominant white culture which insists on knowing best? It seems that different and clashing cultural norms, and the difficulty of understanding those of others, is one of the most serious issues facing the world. We normally think our own values are the correct ones but seeing the world from another point of view is often very illuminating and reveals aspects of life we may not have considered. Just insisting that those who join our national community espouse our values misses the opportunity to learn from theirs.

In the next chapter, I will explore ways in which we might reconcile and transcend these polarising attitudes and how white people can learn from collectivist cultures.

PART 3

....

MAKING PERSONAL AND SOCIETAL CHANGES

....

CHAPTER 7

How Can We Connect White Privilege and Other Forms of Oppression?

Having explored, in the last chapter, how polarising, divisive and conflict-driven our response to different dimensions of culture can be, I will now turn our attention to the objections to understanding and tolerating these differences. I explore what is meant by 'identity politics' and multiculturalism and how the politics tied up with these terms can sometimes reveal a lack of understanding of white privilege. Without an understanding of how white privilege works and how it has profoundly affected the lives of black communities, many white people do not always understand the nature of this issue. Some downplay cultural difference and prefer to have a unified critique of societal ills (Lilla, 2017) with class rather than race at its heart. Other writers see multiculturalism as a 'failed policy' because they see neighbourhoods lacking in cohesion and in conflict with the rest of society (Lennon, 2016). This argument is growing in credibility at the time of writing, particularly as politics is becoming more polarised with the election of Trump to the White House and the Brexit vote in the UK as indicators of a significant shift in attitudes to immigrants.

First, I will explore objections both to 'identity politics' and to multiculturalism. These objections challenge the encouragement and tolerance of different ethnic communities within society, all with their own identity, existing side by side, because these critics think these policies and practices are divisive and self-defeating. I will also explore the notion of intersectionality, which shows the way that differently disadvantaged groups intersect with each other, compounding their lack of privilege. Class differences are also important here and those who are more to the left of European and American politics would say that class is more important than race for criticising societal ills. I will also look at how class intersects with race. To help us navigate and understand these complex issues I also introduce the notion that the term 'ethical sensitivity' can replace the term 'political correctness'.

Identity politics

An underlying given for exploring white privilege is that white people are a discrete group within global society that is more privileged than other racial groups. Feminism and gay activism are based on the same foundational idea – men being more privileged than women and heteronormality being more acceptable than other sexualities. The politics of identifying with specific cultural or societal groups is called 'identity politics' (Lilla, 2017). These differently identified groups include race (including different racial and cultural groups), gender, sexuality, disability, class and so on. Criticism of 'identity politics' comes both from the political right and from the socialist left, but with a different focus.

Multiculturalism

Multiculturalism is similar to 'identity politics' in that it is a policy which supports the existence of different cultural groups within communities living side by side. It has also been criticised as a policy that may have resulted in discreet ethnic groups living completely separate lives to others within the same districts. The original idea of multiculturalism is that these different cultural groups would live together in harmony and in an overarching community which they also feel identified with. Critics of multiculturalism say that this does not happen and that these groups are inward looking and not part of general society. It has been blamed for fragmented and alienated communities and even for resulting in terrorist activities, mainly due to lack of access to education and work; for instance, after the London bombings in 2005 (Lennon, 2016). Even Trevor Phillips, who came from Guyana, called for an end to multiculturalism on these grounds when he was the Head of the UK's Commission for Racial Equality.

Criticism of identity politics and multiculturalism

The critique from the liberal as opposed to socialist left suggests that recognising and encouraging small cultural groups within society to celebrate their own identity fragments the socialist cause, or means that people within each group identity magnify the differences between them. Lilla suggests that identity politics ensures that minority groups remain powerless, implying that socialist politicians are unable to support the very people whose lives they would like to improve as they fail to make common cause with each other (Lilla, 2017). These arguments seem to suggest that cultural minorities could be persuaded to disregard their subjectively important identities and join a left-leaning culture, making common cause with each other. Those advocating this point of view are often white like Mark Lilla, author of *The Once and Future Liberal* (Lilla, 2017). Lilla fails to take into account that denial of difference is in itself illiberal, insulting and unnecessary (Hill Collins & Bilge, 2016). He seems to be expecting all groups to take up a liberal, but nevertheless, white way of understanding the world.

The western, liberal left has a similar point of view and also sees identity politics and multiculturalism as problematic (Lilla, 2017:12). They suggest that they could solve the problem of a divided society by bringing racial minorities into their fold, by trying to co-opt them into (white) society where they would not be met with prejudice. The fragmented nature of so many groups organising themselves around their identity is seen as problematic. People who hold these views cannot claim complete open mindedness and lack of prejudice. The very idea that this might be possible gives the lie to it. We all have our own biases and see the world through our own lens. It is important to understand that sometimes asserting the right to our own sense of identity as a group is the best we can do to survive intact (Hill Collins & Bilge, 2016). It is hard for white people to grasp that community identity in a collectivist culture is more important than individual identity.

A centre right position in the UK would like to find ways to ensure that communities integrate with mainstream, white society. They look to 'citizenship' being taught in schools as an example of encouraging future, integrated citizens and see America as a model for this. In France, there is a legal ban on wearing religious symbols in public in an attempt to integrate society. While this might seem egalitarian as it applies as much to Christians as to Muslims and other beliefs, the wearing of religious symbols such as the burka or turbans can be much more important for people in non-Christian communities, particularly as these are from minorities for whom asserting one's religion is deeply constitutive for the group's sense of identity – an aspect of their spiritual homes and self-identification in another country.

The critique from the ultra-right suggests that we can remove minorities by 'sending them home'. Although those who espouse this view are small in number, this voice is growing louder.

It may be true that multiculturalism and identity politics have not reaped the rewards anti-racists had intended, but this is not because too much difference has been allowed and too much tolerance hoped for. Learning to live with difference, and understanding others' ways are not easy undertakings – as we will see below – but they are possible.

One of the dimensions of cultural difference I mentioned in the last chapter, 'uncertainty avoidance' (Hofstede, 1980), can lead to a situation where one culture attributes general validity to its own culture as the only correct way of being, thinking and behaving (Hill Collins & Bilge, 2016). In the context of this book, I am particularly keen to show that it is incumbent on white, western people to understand that their culture is not the only true culture others should aspire to (Bonnett, 2000; Ryde, 2009), but one among many, and that we may learn by listening to and having a dialogue with others. Although there may be many other cultures who also think theirs is the only true way, it is not our business to be concerned with that as white people, as it is their problem and not ours. Those who have less power may have more reason to cling to a sense of certainty that they are right.

Where I would agree with Lilla regards his critique of the 'hyper-individualistic' society (Lilla, 2017:29) that America has become. This individualism, as I describe in the last chapter, is also to be found in Europe and other places where white Europeans have settled. He shows how Americans often vote for people like Reagan (and Trump) who tell the people that they are fine as they are. They tell the electorate that reliance on your own efforts is what pays off – so do not look beyond your own interest to the way that your own individualistic striving disadvantages others. In other words, look after your own interests and fight only for your own perceived advantage. These politicians realise that, to win elections, they need to show that they want to keep the status quo and not encourage the electorate to look beyond their immediate self-interest. Appearing to criticise those you hope will vote for you is unlikely to pay off!

Politicians who mock political correctness and don't follow its rules have become more popular, particularly as political correctness can be perceived as chastising you for thinking what you think. As I showed in Chapter 3, what is known as 'political correctness', was devised to invent language which is inclusive, respectful and recognises difference. I showed how the insistence on political correctness often has unintended negative consequences and can become counterproductive. In recent years, the term has become increasingly toxic, particularly to people who feel alienated from the political elite. They feel gagged from saying what they 'really think' and, led by the right-wing press, like nothing better than a juicy piece of 'political correctness gone mad' to make fun of. An example from America is from the Urban Dictionary, which defines political correctness as 'a way that we speak in America, so we don't offend whining pussies'. It has become a term many people love to hate, along with rules for 'health and safety' – bureaucrats making up rules that seem to fly in the face of 'common sense'.

It is ironic that people who want to encourage liberal attitudes to diverse communities, and use this term more enthusiastically than many who find it absurd, have to face the fact that it was originally used by the Soviet Union in order to curb free speech and repress dissidents. It makes sense, then, that the idea that the thought police are out to get you is bound to be invoked. Politically correct language is often associated with politicians, bureaucrats and the 'liberal elite', who are accused of liking to tell people how to think and are suspected of feeling contemptuous towards members of the public who are perhaps less liberal (and educationally disadvantaged).

The 'liberal elite' (Luce, 2017) has become a pejorative name for politicians and those who work the machinery of government in centres of power like capital cities. This disparaging term implies that all who work in government are self-serving, contemptuous of 'ordinary' people and out of touch with the lives of those who struggle with the realities of everyday life, particularly those who live outside large urban areas like London and the 'home counties' in the UK and Washington and other east or west coast cities in the USA. The people who use this term see the 'liberal elite' as being left leaning but out of touch with the lives of working-class people.

Intersectionality

Intersectionality is an idea that resolves some of the difficulties mentioned above. It is a way of understanding different oppressive systems as being interconnected and intersecting with each other in their effects on certain people. For example, being oppressed for being black, for being working class or for being female intersect and affect each other (Hill Collins & Bilge, 2016). The nuanced and self-reflective thinking involved in *ethical sensitivity* needs to be present when approaching intersectionality. There are complex issues of who is advantaged and disadvantaged, which can lead to conflict and lack of trust. Many people from working-class communities who struggle to make ends meet object to the idea of white privilege, as they feel far from privileged themselves. The suggestion that they might be privileged is another crazy idea they feel that the liberal elite may foist on them. I have found, since writing my last book (Ryde, 2009), that the very idea of white privilege is often objected to because many white people feel under-privileged themselves. As I showed in Chapter 2, white privilege *is* real and applies to all classes of white people even if some are less privileged than others.

Different minorities such as members of the LGBT (lesbian, gay, bisexual and transgender) community and people with disabilities can be disadvantaged in similarly insidious ways to black people. Belonging to the working class can further exacerbate these disadvantages. These can interdependently compound each other. This phenomenon is usefully called 'intersectionality', which gives us a name to help us to think about the issues involved in being affected by various disadvantages. Hill Collins and Bilge describe intersectionality thus:

Many contemporary definitions of intersectionality emphasize social inequality, but not all do. Intersectionality exists because many people were deeply concerned by the forms of social inequality they either experienced themselves or saw around them. Intersectionality adds additional layers of complexity to understandings of social inequality, recognizing that social inequality is rarely caused by a single factor. Using intersectionality as an analytic tool encourages us to move beyond seeing social inequality through race-only or class-only lenses. Instead, intersectionality encourages understandings of social inequality based on interactions among various categories. (Hill Collins & Bilge, 2016:26)

This does not mean that we can ignore the centrality of white cultural dominance in western societies. White people still benefit by mostly living in a rich part of the world and being advantaged by wealth that is, to a great extent, built on the exploitation of other countries through slavery and colonisation, as I show elsewhere in this book. Poverty is relative and compared to many parts of the world, poor people in white-dominated countries are well off even though it is shocking that some people now have to resort to food banks and sleeping rough or are housed in poor and unhealthy conditions. Many of us are habituated to the fact – and therefore not so shocked by knowing – that many people live in much worse conditions in Africa and India, for example.

Class

So, what is class and how does it intersect with race? The meaning of the term 'working class' has changed over the years. When Karl Marx used it to describe the 'proletariat', it meant those who did not 'own the means of production' (Marx, 2013). The means of production were owned by the 'capitalist class' or the 'upper classes'. The upper classes also contained the aristocracy, who owned wealth through inheriting it. There were therefore three classes: upper, middle and working class. In his book, *Social Class in the 21st Century*, Savage (2015) shows how class differences have changed over the last decades so that the stratification into 'upper, middle and working class' no longer describes the more complex situation we find on the ground. His seven (rather than three) classifications grew out of research he helped to carry out for the BBC called 'The Great British Class Survey'.[3] These seven groupings are:

---

3   www.bbc.co.uk/science/0/21970879

1. elite
2. established middle class
3. technical middle class
4. new affluent
5. traditional working class
6. emerging service workers
7. precariat.

Savage shows how ethnic minorities show up in a complex way within this classification. He says:

> Ethnic minorities are relatively under-represented among the elite, but are well represented in the established middle class beneath them. We also see that ethnic minorities are very well represented among the 'emerging service workers', the group of well-educated young people who have not yet procured large amounts of economic capital. So there appear to be some telling indications here as to how ethnicity is bound up with these new class categories, in that ethnic minorities have considerable amounts of cultural capital but have not been able to translate this into economic capital in the same way that white Britons have. This complex patterning of ethnic minorities into these different new classes is a further indication of the way that ethnic groups cannot be clearly positioned within the older middle/working class divide. (Savage, 2015:173)

He suggests that class is made up of three types of 'capital' (Savage, 2015:4): your wealth and income (economic capital), your tastes, interests and activities (cultural capital) and your social networks, friendships and associations (social capital). He shows clearly how all three types of capital are at play in determining how successful someone is in life. Those who become leaders in government in both politics and public administration are likely to be people who are rich in all three areas. It is no wonder then that people with fewer 'capital' advantages feel alienated by those in power – the liberal elite – however well intentioned and sympathetic to the lives of ordinary people they may be.

Nevertheless, the term 'liberal elite', like 'politically correct', tends to polarise opinion and interfere with more nuanced thinking. Left-leaning politicians are not all out of touch with the lives of their constituents, and many work hard to try to improve their lot, notwithstanding the iron law of oligarchy (Michels, 1915), which shows how inevitably democratic organisations become oligarchies over time (Savage, 2015). Shared advantage often leads to a coterie of people with converging views. This process is not inevitable, and many politicians do successfully engage with the lives of their constituents. By being branded 'liberal elite' as a term of abuse they may turn into popular hate figures, which makes it difficult for well-intentioned individuals to do their job. That is not to say that some people in government do not often lose sight of the lives of less advantaged others: their own higher standard of living and their more privileged education create a privileged horizon which fails to include people with different experience and background. Their privilege can give them the sense that they know better than their constituents.

Jo Cox is an example of a British Member of Parliament (MP) who fell foul of the anger felt by someone who hated political leaders. Her murderer had links to right-wing political parties and she was seen by him to be working towards policies which he believed were the cause of the world's problems. She was a passionate believer in the European Union and worked to help all immigrants, including refugees and asylum seekers, and had a particular interest in Middle Eastern countries, especially Syria, having worked for Oxfam before becoming an MP.

Jo Cox could be seen as a typical member of the 'liberal elite'. In spite of being born into a working-class family, she went to grammar school and then to Cambridge and started her working career as a political adviser. She worked tirelessly for her constituents in Batley and Spen in Yorkshire, England, a traditional working-class community, and her home was in the constituency. No doubt her murderer hated any idea of what he saw as political correctness.

Jeremy Corbyn, who could certainly not be accused of abandoning ordinary people, could, nevertheless be called a member of the liberal elite. His life has been dedicated to serving disadvantaged people and standing up for minorities. However, he represents the wealthy London borough of Islington and came from a relatively middle-class family in the west of England. Generic terms like 'liberal elite' or, indeed, 'the chattering classes' can mislead and generate polarisation.

Ethical sensitivity

So how can a more tolerant attitude to difference be generated without driving prejudiced thoughts underground? How can we take into account that we may be driven by unconscious or not clearly conscious attitudes and biases? As I suggested above, if this attitude needs a name to replace 'political correctness', we could call it 'ethical sensitivity'. Ethical sensitivity comes into play when we sense that an ethical dilemma is present that needs careful attention. For instance, it is our ethical sensitivity that alerts us, as white people, to a racist thought we have and leads us to be thoughtful about it rather than take it at face value or bat it away as shameful. It helps us to be reflective regarding our responses to black people and the 'automatic' thoughts we have – those that seem to arise unbidden. With ethical sensitivity, we don't chide ourselves for having thoughts that seem to go against our espoused views. We can think about where these thoughts come from – do they arise from prejudice or irrational fear or taught responses, or something else? With this reflective attitude, it becomes easier (though never completely easy) not to be defensive. We understand that our conscious selves are not always in charge of all our thoughts.

Ethical sensitivity is similar to, or an aspect of, ethical maturity (Carroll & Shaw, 2013). As with ethical sensitivity, there are no moral rules to follow in ethical maturity. Instead, we are guided by ethical principles that help us to understand the complexity often present within ethical dilemmas and use those principles to influence our actions. Carroll and Shaw show how difficult that is and how they and all of us fall short again and again. They say, for example, 'I hate fundamentalism, but is that itself a fundamentalist stance? I like to think I am liberal but am not quite sure if that just reflects my white, middle-class values' (Carroll & Shaw, 2013).

A triad of privileges

In order to understand privilege with ethical sensitivity, we do not have to decide who is the most privileged. We have established that we can be privileged in one area but not in another. In order to understand privilege in a more nuanced way, we could consider three areas of privilege: cultural, social and educational. These are similar though not entirely the same as the three areas of cultural capital found by Savage (2015). Expressed diagrammatically the situation may look like this:

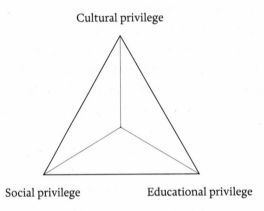

Figure 7.1: A triad of privileges

- *Cultural privilege* is the privilege conferred on people because of their dominant race. I am referring mostly to white privilege, which I have described more fully in other chapters. Within non-white groups, privilege often comes with being 'more like' or able to 'pass' as white, such as those with lighter coloured skins and similar facial features or hair. This is sometimes described as 'shadeism' or 'colourism' (Webb, 2017).
- *Social privilege* is the privilege conferred by being a member of the most advantaged social class. This used to be the upper class as the most privileged group, followed by the middle class, but now includes the classes identified by Savage as 'elite', as the top class, followed by the 'established middle class'. Class privilege often, but not necessarily, comes with wealth, a comfortable lifestyle and greater access to jobs and education. Accent, style of dressing and ways of behaving are often signifiers of social privilege (Savage, 2015).
- *Educational privilege* is conferred by access to higher education. This not only provides a source of knowledge but also skills for accessing knowledge. It often leads to a greater scope for choices in life, including careers and a greater access to influential networks and knowledge of the arts and literature.

Those who are privileged in any of the three areas often find it hard to recognise that they are privileged, since we all tend to take our own status for granted.

Those who are *culturally privileged* (particularly white people) tend not to see their privilege but to see those from black and minority ethnic groups as 'other', as different – not the norm – having a 'race' where they do not. Often those who have physical characteristics that are close to white people are advantaged above those who do not. I wonder, for instance, if Barack Obama would have become President of the United States if he had had a more 'African' appearance.

Those who are *socially privileged* tend to take this for granted and regard those without that privilege as simply uncouth or ignorant. This privilege often comes with educational privilege as socially privileged people often can afford a good education. Socially privileged people – in other words those from higher social classes – can signal their dominance by the way they speak and dress and the ease with which they approach socially privileged situations.

Those who have *educational privilege* may also have social privilege as they can afford a good education, but this is not necessarily the case. They may have won a scholarship to a 'good' school rather than been able to afford it. Those without educational privilege will often use simpler words or the 'wrong' word or pronunciation according to those who are educationally privileged. A well-educated person may well see those who have not been given this privilege as somehow not bright or able. The less educated may not be able to signal their erudition by referring to classical literature, the latest book to win the Booker prize or classical music and opera. They are more likely to refer to 'popular' culture such as television programmes and music. While both may mock or even despise the other, the more educated person is more likely to feel superior and the less educated, inferior – even while in real-life terms both groups are habituated to their specific culture. The more educated person can signal his or her education and sophistication to others, including potential employers, by mentioning books, plays or music that impress, and speaking in a more articulate way.

Some people have all three of these privileges, which confers multiple privilege. There are also many who lack cultural privilege but are rich in the other two and those who lack educational and social privilege but are rich in cultural privilege. None of these privileges invalidates the other. The way these different privileges interface with each other is another example of intersectionality. Attempting to assert that lacking one is worse than lacking the other is fruitless. They are all important disadvantages and it is common for someone who is disadvantaged in one area to be disadvantaged in another, but it is not inevitable. There are many well-educated and 'sophisticated' black people. This does not mean that their being black does not negatively impact their lives in a predominantly white society at all. For instance, the black ornithologist J. Drew Lanham found himself unable to do his field research when he came upon a house with a Republican flag and a dog barking. Images of lynching parties came to him forcefully (Lanham, 2017). This book focuses on the cultural privilege of white people but does not deny that the other two privileges exist and have a significant effect on the lives of the people who are in some way disadvantaged – and this includes people from ethnic minorities as well as the white majority.

In this chapter, I have shown how thinking about social privilege is complex and that ethical sensitivity is more helpful than the rules of political correctness to help us navigate these choppy waters. The move to vilify 'identity politics' can be a way of denying and denigrating differences rather than celebrating and embracing them. Intersectionality helps us to think in a more nuanced way about how different privileges intersect and do not have to be pitted against each other. Having explored the complexities of the different ways privilege can be understood, I now want to address this question: Is there an underlying or overarching philosophy that will help us to understand white privilege and how to transcend it? In the next chapter, we will explore how a systemic and participatory worldview will help us towards this.

CHAPTER 8

Towards a Systemic and Participatory Worldview

So far, I have established the following:

- White people are privileged because they constitute the norm in western countries and socially benefit from historically accumulated wealth.
- This can be denied for a variety of reasons.
- Attempts to tackle racism have not been successful.

So how can we be more successful in reducing denial and encourage a clear-sighted view of our own culpability as white people along with genuinely tolerant attitudes? One of the urgent issues of the day is how we reconcile apparently conflicting positions. This includes understanding each other's cultural viewpoints but also addressing inequalities of power and wealth. Insisting on such egalitarian practices through rules and laws, and disparaging those who seem to be intolerant, is not working and, at times, is even counterproductive.

In view of the urgency of finding an answer to (racial) inequality in western societies and between nations worldwide, what will help us reconcile the difference between individualistic and collectivist cultures (see Chapter 5) which now encounter each other – and what will reduce the polarisation between the two?

It is my view that we need a complete change in the way we understand our world, a change in epistemology which views it as interconnected and interdependent even where we are apparently different. In this way, we might make more real headway in finding pathways towards reconciliation, which includes white people facing their privilege and accepting appropriate responsibility. This change towards a systemic epistemology is gaining recognition in fields as far apart as science, philosophy, psychotherapy and spirituality. Hawkins (2018) has written extensively about systemic thinking which, he says, shows how we cannot separate ourselves from our environment. He calls this way of constructing the world and our perceptions 'participative systemic thinking' and describes it thus:

> [Participative systems thinking] arises from the realization that I can never see a system objectively, for by studying a system I create a new system which connects the studied and the studier, in which both affect the other. The bicycle and rider are affected by the audience that is cheering them on, timing their journey or asking them questions. You can never see the totality of a system that you are part of, for you will always see that system from the perspective of your position within it. (Hawkins, 2018)

Peter Reason, Emeritus Professor in the Business School of the University of Bath, who is also an ecologist and nature writer, uses the term 'participatory world view' (Reason, 1994), by which he means, one which sees that all is interconnected. We are not separate individuals, as is suggested in Descartes' dualistic theory of 'I think therefore I am', stipulating an essential separateness between the subject and object of perception, but in systemic approaches, everything is intimately and inevitably part of the other. Those who accept a participative worldview know that *I cannot view any part of the world without myself affecting it*. Reason and Bradbury say: 'Within this perspective, human persons are centres of consciousness both independent and linked in a generative web of communication, both with other humans and with the rest of creation' (Reason & Bradbury, 2001:8).

In psychotherapeutic and psychoanalytic theorising, systemic inter-subjectivists (Stolorow & Atwood, 1992) have a similar view, in which the nature of the self shows up differently, depending on the systemic context in which people are situated. My nature changes when I relate to different people in different circumstances. In this view, the self is not an autonomous separate unit. It exists within a cultural and interpersonal matrix. In other words, we all exist within an interconnected system and cannot be extracted from it. Here are some quotes from theorists from quite different disciplines which assert that individuals do not really exist as such. This is one from the psychoanalytic discipline of intersubjective systems theory (IST):

> The assumptions of traditional psychoanalysis have been pervaded by the Cartesian doctrine of the isolated mind. This doctrine bifurcates the subjective world of the person into outer and inner regions, reifies and absolutises the resulting separation between the two, and pictures the mind as an objective entity that takes its place among other objects, a 'thinking thing', that has an inside with contents and looks out on an external world from which it is essentially estranged. (Stolorow & Atwood, 1992)

From field theory:

> The field is a whole in which the parts are in immediate relationship and responsive to each other and no part is uninfluenced by what goes on elsewhere in the field. (Yontef, 1993)

From dialogic gestalt theory:

> At the heart of this approach is the belief that the ultimate basis of our existence is relational or dialogic in nature: we are all threads in an interhuman fabric. (Hycner & Jacobs, 1995)

If we look again at the difference between individualistic and collectivist cultures, but this time include a third column where this systemic epistemology is placed, we can transcend the polarity between the two.

We can see from Table 8.1 that neither individualistic nor collectivist cultures are systemic or participatory in their construction. The lenses through which individualistic cultures look see the individual as the basic unit of society, while collectivism sees the family, group or community as the basic unit. Both imply separation and have boundaries keeping subject and object separate and are part of 'entity thinking' (Hawkins, 2017a). A collectivist view does nevertheless understand that individuals arise within their context and are an inextricable part of it. Other communities and families are separate, however, and not included. The identified group becomes the entity opposed to other entities.

Table 8.1: Values and assumptions with systemic understanding

Values and assumptions	Individualistic cultures	Collectivist cultures	Systemic understanding
The unit of society is	The individual	The family or community	Indivisible
Individuals	Should develop themselves as far as they can – in Maslow's (2014) terms 'self-actualise'	Should work towards the good of their family or community	Do not exist except within relationships or within systemic contexts
The self	Is something that 'belongs' to an individual	Cannot be extricated from a group identity	Is fluid and only exists within relationship
Authenticity is	Important as we have a 'true' self and it is vital to be true to it	About honouring the collective context and your role within it	Co-created through relationships
Membership of community	Is there to support individual well-being	Is there to support the well-being of the tribe	Is the medium in which the individual forms and changes
Psychotherapy, counselling and healing	Help people to know themselves more deeply and resolve personal difficulties and conflicts	Stresses the connections within relationship – often in the context of ancestors, and frequently within a religious or spiritual context	Is undertaken within the awareness of the context of a web of relating on all levels

Systemic thinking has two important aspects. One is that we cannot subtract ourselves from a field of inquiry and observe it 'objectively'. We are inevitably part of any 'field' we observe. The other is that, understood systemically, all systems are interconnected and 'nested' within each other. Those who purport to examine 'a system' are not being truly 'systemic' as they regard themselves as separate from the system they examine. Entity thinking therefore encourages a split between inner and outer, us and them, good and bad, and leads to conflicts where the apparent opposites meet (Hawkins, 2017b).

This systemic way of understanding the world throws white people's sense of themselves as authors of their own fate in doubt. It is quite a challenge to understand this, particularly for those from individualistic cultures where personal authenticity is much prised and approved of. Within the systemic epistemology, authenticity is always co-created through relationship rather than seen as something you 'have' as an individual. Hawkins (2018, in press) describes the implications of this systemic construction of authenticity:

> We need to create a relational, purposive and dynamic notion of authenticity. I suggest that this relational-purposive-dynamic model of authenticity is one where the individual is present in each moment, attempting to align: within themselves; between themselves and individual others; with the wider group; and with collective purpose.

Understanding the world in an atomised way, one in which experience is made up of separate things, we tend to make preferences and divide the world into things we like and approve of and those we reject. Conflict inevitably arises between those who take one side or another of a polarity. If one is good, the other is inevitably bad. Conflict resolution is eased once we can loosen the hold on our rigid opinions and realise that each isolated pole inevitably encapsulates a limited view. This more encompassing way of realising that both constructions may be valid and may facilitate living more peacefully with others. It does not mean that we cannot take a principled stand against someone or something that we disagree with (as I do here in challenging white privilege) but it does mean that we are prepared to listen to other views and be prepared to be wrong.

Although this may seem to be yet another white way of seeing the world, these ideas are recognised in various non-white contexts. For instance, we find it in southern Africa, where the concept of 'ubuntu' is prevalent and has also become well known in the West in the context of South African reconciliation work. It is an idea which speaks of the interconnectedness of all life and roughly translated means 'I am because we are' or 'I am incomplete without you'. In other words, 'I can only be who I am because we are part of each other' (Tutu & Tutu, 2014:150). It is a philosophy which leads to ethical and empathetic relating and was a guiding principle for Archbishop Desmond Tutu when he led South Africa's Truth and Reconciliation process (Tutu, 1998). Martin Luther King echoed this in a letter he sent from jail in Birmingham, Alabama:

> All I'm saying is simply this: that all life is interrelated, and in a real sense we are all caught in an inescapable network of mutuality, tied in a single garment of destiny. Whatever affects one directly, affects all indirectly. For some strange reason, I can never be what I ought to be until you are what you ought to be. And you can never be what you ought to be until I am what I ought to be. This is the interrelated structure of reality. (Rieder, 2013)

Systemic understanding is also prefigured in mystical traditions such as Buddhism and Sufism, originally found in the Far and Middle East and India. These traditions understand experience as indivisible and interconnected. The Buddhist teacher Thich Nhat Hanh expresses this in his use of the word 'interbeing' (Hanh, 2017). He says: 'If the twentieth century was characterised by individualism and consumption, the twenty first century can be characterised by insight and interconnectedness, and new forms of solidarity and togetherness.'

This way of seeing is often expressed poetically as it is hard to express in prose. The poet Mevlana Jalal Al-Din Rumi, better known in the West as simply Rumi, wrote many poems reaching for a way of expressing the oneness of all.

Inquiry and dialogue

There are two practices and processes that have emerged from understanding the world in this systemic, interconnected way. One is 'inquiry' and the other 'dialogue', though both are connected.

Inquiry, as a methodology, is an in-depth search into a particular subject or experience. It is based on open questions which do not close down the search but seek to open out into possible new questions. Finding the 'right answer' is less important than finding greater depth to the question and other questions that arise through the inquiry. As Otto Scharmer says in his book, *Theory U*, in true dialogue we can approach each other with 'an open mind, open heart and open will' (Scharmer, 2009: 396). For instance, when I was undertaking research for my doctorate, I organised a 'co-operative inquiry' (Reason & Bradbury, 2001) by getting a group of white psychotherapists together to carry out an in-depth inquiry into our experience of being white. This is described more fully in *Being White in the Helping Professions* (Ryde, 2009:56). An example from our work together was our inquiry into our own experience of guilt and shame about being white in the context of the white history of exploiting others. Allowing ourselves to experience those feelings of guilt and shame in ourselves, and express them to each other, led us to understand more deeply how complicit we are in white privilege. This led me to devise the 'white awareness model' (Ryde, 2009) which I discuss in the next chapter.

Dialogue is a similar methodology to inquiry but implies two or more people inquiring together. In my last book, I wrote:

> Several authors have used the word [dialogue]...including Bohm (1996) and Buber (2004). Dialogue involves us in listening to and understanding what is being communicated, even if we think we disagree, even if we think the speaker represents something we thoroughly disapprove of. We listen without forming a repost or even a reply. We listen in order to understand thoroughly. In order to really do this, we may need to check out that we have understood correctly or deeply enough. When we respond, we do so by giving our thoughts and feelings to the speaker, thoughts that have been sparked by what has been said. We are prepared to be hesitant or wrong or foolish because we are more interested in our questions than in finding answers. We think, can my question be deepened by hearing what this person has to say? And can my understanding be deepened? While we are in dialogue we notice what is going on in ourselves while the process of the dialogue is happening. If we find that we have a judgment about that, we notice that too. We bring a sense of witness to what is said so we have no expectations of a particular outcome, other than to have learnt more. We don't mind if our point of view does not 'win'. (Ryde, 2009:59)

Patricia Hill Collins, in the book *Intersectionality* (Hill Collins & Bilge, 2016), also recommends a dialogic approach which does not seek to gloss over differences but, through dialogue, achieves a generative meeting – in other words, one which results in something worthwhile and productive, without the aim of 'winning'. She says:

> Dialogical education offers a useful avenue for how intersectionality might better navigate differences. Using intersectional frameworks to rethink social inequality requires a more participatory and democratic methodology that rejects neoliberal tendencies to assess knowledge based on its 'use' or 'function' for one's individual project. Instead, dialogical education takes on the hard work of developing critical consciousness by talking and listening to people who have different points of view. When it comes to grappling with social inequality, this idea of dialogical education might also help think through some of the challenges that intersectionality faces with methodology. Rather than downplaying or dismissing differences, an intersectional methodology requires negotiating differences that exist within discrete scholarly and political traditions of race, class, gender, sexuality, ability, nationality, ethnicity, colonialism, religion, and immigration. This dialogical methodology assumes no preformatted connection between them. The goal is to make those connections within specific social contexts. Hence, intersectionality's heuristic is a starting point for building intellectual coalitions of consensus and contestation. This dialogical approach would see conflict as an inevitable outcome of bona fide differences *and strive to make them generative*. (Hill Collins & Bilge, 2016:168) (my emphasis)

To propose a dialogic approach in this book which has at its heart a challenge to white people about how they benefit from unacknowledged privilege may seem strange. In asserting that we need to let go of polarised attitudes, this does not undermine this position or let white people 'off the hook'. What it does do is to show a way forward which is less likely to maintain a conflict that is never resolved but flip-flops from one position to the next and eventually erupts either in violence or repression. It is a harder path for white people to take than simply asking them to 'try' to accept that we are privileged and put rules and laws in place which attempt to ensure tolerance and fair practices. We have been down that road and it can easily lead to a backlash, as I have shown. White people may be compliant, and even conscientiously think they understand, but have not really 'bought into' the positions I believe are necessary for progress.

Lynne Jacobs (2016) in her paper, 'Dialogue and double consciousness', proposes four helpful reminders to white people that can aid us on this difficult road. She devised these to help her as a white psychotherapist working with black clients. It seems to me that these requirements equally apply to any social relating. Here is a shortened version of these attitudes that I have created which I find help the dialogue:

1. Bracket my wish to be seen as an individual and remember that I am also a member of a group that lives racistly situated in a dominant position.
2. Remember that if I position myself as innocent, I do not renounce my privilege (pretend it does not exist).
3. Lean into emotional courage to embrace shame and guilt. I do not believe that shame and guilt are *per se* the problem. We need our guilt and our shame.
4. Pay attention to my white culture, my conflict-avoiding orientation and my innocent optimism. These common whiteness traits spring from the confident belonging that feels as sure as a birthright. (Jacobs, 2016)

In the next chapter, I will look further at how we can understand our own whiteness beyond a conceptual grasp. I will offer a model which helps white people to understand their position in a more fundamental way. We may then be able to relate authentically to each other, to different groups and to wider systemic levels within a multiracial and multicultural world.

CHAPTER 9

How to Uncover Your Own Whiteness

I n the last chapter, I explored how to find more effective ways of overcoming polarised attitudes to cultural difference, based on different ways of under-standing the world. In this chapter, I will explore how individuals can make this more of a reality within their daily lives. This chapter speaks particularly to white people, though black people may be interested in our exploration.

In considering these matters there is a tendency to talk in general terms about how attitudes could change. However persuasive these arguments are, they are unlikely to lead to actual change, as changing in practice is a lot more difficult than thinking about it. So, can we, as white people (if we are white) fundamentally change in such a way that we understand what our whiteness means and how our attitudes and behaviours contribute to a racist society? As in my last book, *Being White in the Helping Professions* (Ryde, 2009), I suggest that we can only begin to effect change if we start with ourselves.

Much of my last book laid out how hard it is for white people to understand that whiteness *is* a race within a racialised context (Ryde, 2009). Of course, it is now well known that race is a social rather than biological concept (Alcoff, 2015:21; Dalal, 2002:ch 8) but within society it is all too present and white people are not neutral observers (Bonnett, 2000:120; Dyer, 1997). Race is not only a matter for those who are not white. Furthermore, white people's denial that they have a race is part of the problem, particularly as being white bestows privileges, as we saw in Chapter 2. That white people are *able* not to think about race is itself a privilege – and also a problem. In her moving and honest book, *Waking Up White*, Debby Irving describes the way she discovered her racial whiteness, and she has a very instructive story:

> [at school] we'd been asked to fill out a survey. One of the questions went something like this: How often do you talk about race with your family and friends? Daily, once a week, once a month, a couple times a year, never? I went back and forth between 'once a month' and 'a couple times a year,' thinking, who talks about race daily? All of the students of color answered 'daily.' I couldn't believe it. I couldn't even fathom what there would be to talk about every day. I didn't yet understand that not talking about race was a privilege available only to white people. (Irving, 2014)

This was certainly true for me and it was brought home to me sharply when my fellow doctoral students at the University of Bath in the UK said that research into intercultural issues was not for me as I was white. This shock awakened in me a realisation that my whiteness is also part of the cultural context in which race is found. I described in my book the way that I, as an en-raced person, gradually appeared like a picture slowly emerging from a blank page (Ryde, 2009).

This situation is infuriating for non-whites as the level of denial and blindness to the influence and effects of being white on society is so very clearly marked from a non-white perspective. It led Eddo-Lodge to write the book *Why I'm No Longer Talking to White People About Race* (2017), a title that captures attention and expresses the frustration well!

My research led me to devise a process for owning and exploring our own attitudes to whiteness. The model builds on another, the Helms Identity model. Like mine, Helms's model shows a period of denial, an ignorance or acceptance of the status quo, a period of struggle and disintegration followed by a more thorough understanding which she calls 'autonomy'. This model does not include feelings of guilt and shame, which I think is necessary to effect real change and I show why this is the case below. It is a circular model which goes from Denial; Establishing a new openness and a new equality with the other; Guilt and shame; Owning up to my own white privilege; to Integration.

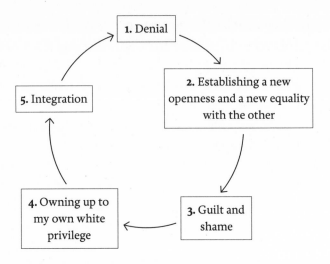

Figure 9.1: The White Awareness Model (Ryde, 2009:134)

So how does the White Awareness Model help people understand and overcome their racist attitudes? It has been devised as a circular process that can be moved around in several iterations. Someone may start at different points, as I outlined above, and move to another point in the cycle but return to another level of denial. There may be greater understanding at this point but also some way to go. It is also possible to try to miss out stages but, in my view, this does not lead to real change.

I have, myself, experienced this process of going around the cycle several times; for instance, before, during and at the end of my research; before during and at the end of writing my previous book; and between writing my last book and this one. In all these journeys round the cycle, a more profound realisation about white privilege has come to me.

We will now discuss the different stopping points on the cycle.

1. Denial

The starting point is at number 1, where denial of the problem is located. This denial can have many levels depending on the degree of awareness of white privilege present in the inquirer. Greater racism does not necessarily mean more denial of white privilege. A very racist person may not deny their white privilege but certainly not be interested in understanding and remedying what this means to non-white people within a racialised society. Levels of denial are as follows:

1. *White pride:* 'I am proud of being white – white people have improved the world considerably, but this is a white country and those who are black should not be allowed to live here. They can go back to where they came from.' Denial that racism is harmful is present and, at this level of racism, being white may be thought of as a good thing.

2. *Race is not an issue for me:* This stage has less hostility, but denial is definitely present: 'I don't think that being white is anything that affects me or is important. The colour of my skin isn't even really white – it is sort of pinkish.'

3. *Some of them are okay.* This stage expresses hostility but denies its intensity. 'I don't much like foreigners and think we should limit the number coming here as they take our jobs and houses, but some of them are okay. I know a few black people and I am not racist. They are okay.'

4. *Colour-blind*: This stage has less denial. The stance of a 'colour-blind' person is to say: 'I am white, but I have many black friends. I am colour-blind. Being white doesn't really affect me – I am not racist.' It is possible that someone with a colour-blind stance might come to understand the position of black people and move on to the next level of 'Establishing a new openness and a new equality with the other.' This might drive more awareness and a desire to explore further. It might also bring them to a *Liberal angst* position of denial.

5. *Liberal angst*: This stage is well meaning and full of white guilt but tries to short-cut the road to full white awareness. Those with liberal angst say, 'I am white and realise I have an easier time in society because of it, but I always make sure that I challenge racist remarks and that anti-racist policies are put in place where I work.' People at this level of denial are the most likely to move on to the next stage of 'Establishing a new openness and a new equality with the other.'

People with these ways of understanding what it means to live in a racialised society are all at the first position on the White Awareness Model – that of Denial. The number 5 level of denial – *Liberal angst* – as I have said, is the most likely to move to the next stage, maybe through conversations with friends or colleagues or through reading. Those at the *Colour-blind* level of denial could also move to this stage or move to a *Liberal angst* position. This could also occur by having their views challenged and dialogically explored.

I can, myself, identify with this move. When my Nigerian school friend mentioned in Chapter 1 rejected me and our other school friends, it had a profound effect on my realisation of what it meant to be black and subject to processes of 'othering'. Nevertheless, I think I only moved to the *Liberal angst* position and did not really fully embrace the next stage of the model until I started my doctorate research.

The first of these four, *White pride*, is clearly racist and while people with these views may be few, their number is clearly increasing in Europe and America with far-right parties gaining in popularity. As I write, the British Labour Party is also struggling to distance itself from members who have written shockingly racist remarks about Jewish people. We saw in the last chapter that there may be more people who espouse racist opinions than is immediately obvious, as they may only express them to people whom they know hold similar views, as we saw revealed by police officers when filmed by an undercover reporter (see Chapter 2). However, with the widespread use of social media, there have been massive changes in the way that people communicate such racist views in recent years, and these can now more easily be revealed in society beyond a few friends. Where in the past we may have been unaware of racist views held by people we do not know, we are now more aware of them though social media – and even the unconsidered tweets of the President of the USA.

The second, *Race is not an issue for me*, is much more common. There is not so much overt hostility to black people but more a lack of interest in the issues. People who hold these views tend not to value thinking about society and its ills. They take life as it comes and often use humour to keep uncomfortable thoughts and feelings at arm's-length.

People in the third denial category, *Some of them are okay*, do think about society but are fearful of change. They see immigrants as a threat. They are often impoverished themselves and fear that immigrants will deprive them of the country's resources such as jobs and housing. They may well be aware that many individual immigrants are good people and are at pains to deny the charge of racism.

Those in the fourth position, *Colour-blind,* lack understanding of the privilege bestowed by being white and the difficulties that black people have in society. People who hold these views are at pains to show that they are not racist and would prefer to avoid conflict.

The fifth position, *Liberal angst,* is more thoughtful and people here make a genuine attempt not to be racist but do not fully take the wider considerations of what it means to be white into account. People in this fifth position are genuinely well intentioned but fail to understand the depth of the issues. They tend to see the problem as one that can be fixed by altering laws and rules governing society.

My guess is that Eddo-Lodge (2017) is writing for the *Colour-blind* and *Liberal angst* groups – those who are well intentioned but do not 'get it'. I imagine from what she says in her book that she is particularly angry with white people in these two groups who do not 'get it' but think that they do. Some of us white people who are politically aware can be very arrogant about our level of understanding of the experience of black people. This can be in spite, or even because, of our political involvement where our identity is passionately caught up with being right.

2. Establishing a new openness and a new equality with the other

As we face up to our layers of denial we may then engage with the *Establishing a new openness and a new equality with the other* position. I use the word 'struggle' as it always is a struggle to really understand another, particularly when their experience of the world is so different from our own. As we saw in other chapters, it is hard to understand others without being defensive and wanting to justify ourselves. This struggle may involve reading books and watching films or television programmes that show the effects of racism, talking to black people and discussing these matters with friends and colleagues. Open, generative dialogues in which there is genuine desire to understand and a curiosity to really know others' experience are needed for this stage to be successful enough that the next stage can be reached.

3. Guilt and shame

It is often hard for people to understand why I consider this to be an important part of this strategy for change. Black people often say they are not interested in hearing about white people's sense of guilt and shame. That is because it is often offered to them as if the white person was saying: 'Please absolve me of my guilt. I recognise that white people have been guilty of harming you and I am truly sorry about it.' White guilt is not a matter for black people to hear about and be interested in. Nor are they able to absolve us as this is a societal issue and, as I show below, involves reparation which goes further than words. Non-white people are more interested in change than confessions of guilt and shame. However, I do think that white people must recognise that they are guilty, both in their personal lives and because their forbears and politicians who represent them in the past and in the present day are, and have been, guilty of unspeakable crimes against those who are not white and we are still living off the fruits of this exploitation.

Just one example is the triangular route that slavers took (Hirsch, 2018; Olusoga, 2016), carrying slaves from Africa to America, raw materials from America to Britain and manufactured goods from Britain to Africa. This infamous trade made many parts and aspects of white society very rich indeed – wealth we are still benefiting from which forms part of the basis of our privileged and wealthy societies today (Hirsch, 2018). The callousness, cruelty and carelessness with which other human lives were treated is very shocking. This seems even worse in the context of white people's supreme self-confidence in thinking they are occupying the pinnacle of achievement to which others should aspire. This kind of thinking leads white people to become involved in wars such as the one in Iraq which did untold damage and also the 'war on terror' where the 'enemy' is not even identified correctly (Iraq was not behind the 9/11 attacks and did not have weapons of mass destruction). This leads to great human rights abuses and miscarriages of justice.

Other examples from recent times include imprisonment without trial in Guantanamo Bay where many innocent people were held (Worthington, 2015), as well as the forced deportation of asylum seekers to countries where they may be tortured or their lives may be in danger (Amnesty International, 2018).

If these matters are really taken on board and understood, what white person can avoid feeling guilty and ashamed? It is not self-indulgent or wrongheaded or something that 'bleeding-heart liberals' do out of 'soft' thinking. It is a deep human response to the reality of being involved in something shockingly harmful. I point out in my research (Ryde, 2009:ch 3) that guilt is not really a feeling. Guilt arises when we decide something is a matter of fact or not. Do we plead guilty or not guilty of some misdemeanour? If we decide that we are guilty, then a feeling of shame arises, and this feeling alerts us to something being amiss that needs to be put right. If we are guilty and feel ashamed, then it is incumbent on us to make reparations. I discuss this in Chapter 12.

In my doctorate research on which my last book was based, I carried out an inquiry, both into the nature of guilt and shame and into these feelings experienced by white people. Most of those I interviewed as part of a research group felt ashamed of the ways in which they personally had been racist. For instance, some expressed feeling ashamed because they automatically felt fear when they saw a black man walking towards them in the street, but they did not feel guilty for the racist policies of their elected leaders or for the events carried out many decades ago by white forebears who they could not have personally influenced.

The more we explored the ways in which we still benefit by racist policies the more prepared my co-researchers and I were to feel ashamed of past events and to see the way in which we are personally implicated.

4. Owning up to my own white privilege

Realising guilt and shame brings us to the next point, which is the struggle to understand our unseen, culturally determined, attitudes and unconscious biases. Recognising our guilt and the feeling of shame carries us to this point. We are now taking the focus fully onto ourselves rather than seeing the problem of racism as belonging to the other, thinking that this is for black people to deal with. This is a huge step for a white person to take and one that is not encouraged in the unthinking way in which people in the white world operate – one of supreme racial self-confidence. It can involve the hard work of finding out about the history of white people and colonisation – how they came to be as rich as they are without assuming it was just cleverness, ingenuity and sophisticated thinking.

As well as this 'thinking' work there is something even more difficult, which is self-exploration. From my research I discovered, both in myself and my co-researchers, that white people frequently have racist thoughts. Many of these are so fleeting that they are hard to capture. During my research and, since then, in my teaching, I have encouraged people to become aware of these thoughts and allow them into their consciousness. Most people do not like to own them, but they are influencing us all of the time. Some examples are:

- 'How has a black person managed to buy a car like that?'
- 'I bet he has children but doesn't bring them up himself.'
- 'Oh, her father was black, no wonder she has father issues.'
- 'Black women are unfriendly, they never smile at you.'
- 'How great that a black person can become the president.'

It is hard for white people to own these thoughts and I have taken to congratulating them if they find one. It is counterintuitive to bring them to the front of the mind, but, in my view, it is the best, and maybe only, way to see and understand the extent to which racist assumptions are active underground and the way in which these racist thoughts affect us in our daily lives.

You, as the reader, might like to consider whether you have had any of these thoughts. I have/have had all of the ones mentioned above, which is why they occur to me now! You might also like to think of other racist thoughts that come to you.

5. Integration

The fifth and last stage of this model is integration. Here the white person understands the depths and implications of their whiteness without having to deny their history or feelings. They recognise their own racism, are thoughtful about it, and owning of it, so that they are less likely to be unthinkingly racist. They can relate to others within a racial environment without carelessly seeing themselves as racially neutral and, with this acknowledgement, they are more prepared to make reparation or make moves to do so. This knowing of one's white racial identity and not being in denial of what it means within a racialised society helps us to live in our own skin and relate to non-white people in a more straightforward way. At this point, or in the future, the person may again become aware of denied racism and the cycle can be gone through again, maybe in more depth this time.

The model when looked at from a specifically white awareness context can now look like this:

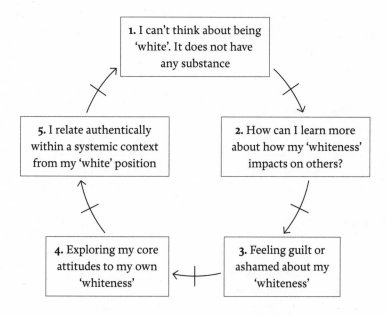

Figure 9.2: Blocks to moving round the White Awareness Model

Moving to each position on the cycle is not easy and there are typical blocks interfering with making the movement. Here are the kinds of difficulties which might arise:

Denial → Establishing a new openness and a new equality with the other. Making this move involves owning up to the denial present, and that is always difficult as it means owning up to having been wrong. This can feel undermining to our sense of identity. Sometimes it is coming across some information – such as a book or television programme – about what it is like to be a non-white person in a predominantly white world that can lead to the move away from denial.

Establishing a new openness and a new equality with the other→ Guilt and shame. This move is particularly difficult as guilt and shame can feel like an assault on the sense of oneself as a 'good person'. It is easy to think that all that is necessary in making us more white aware is to have a theoretical understanding of it. But if the move into these difficult feelings is not made, then the struggle to understand other perspectives just leads to another kind of denial, and maybe the move could be towards *liberal angst,* for example. Typically, then, the move might look like this: *Denial (colour-blind) → Establishing a new openness and a new equality with the other → Denial (liberal angst).*

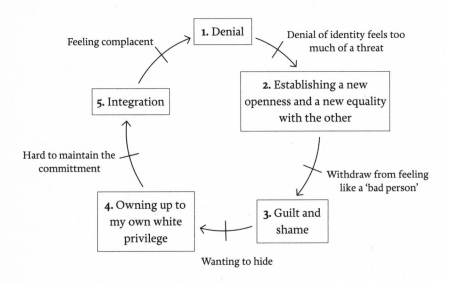

Figure 9.3: Blocks to engaging in the White Awareness Model

Guilt and shame → Owning up to my own white privilege. This move could also send us back to the previous position as we might find it too painful. Typically, we might want to hide from our complicity by being more interested in our theoretical understanding than really owning our own part in it and moving forward.

Owning up to my own white privilege → Integration. This move is hard to make as we might just touch on self-exploration and not be sufficiently thorough to reach a sense of integration. Staying open enough to continue with self-exploration can be arduous and requires a commitment to stay focused on it.

If we put these blocks to moving round the cycle diagrammatically, it would look like Figure 9.3:

Some exercises to discover your own whiteness

As a trainer in counselling, psychotherapy and supervision, I often teach people to work across cultures, particularly as I have a speciality in working with refugees and asylum seekers. As I set out on writing this book, and for my last book, I was keen that the white people within these groups did not just focus on 'other' cultures. I wanted to challenge the, often tacit, idea that other people 'have' a race while they are racially neutral. For this teaching, I use various methods for helping white people to know themselves racially and become aware of their, often denied, racism. This will include engaging with the White Awareness Model as a way of working towards a fuller awareness of their own whiteness.

Here are some exercises I introduce to white people. I have grouped them around the stages of the White Awareness Model.

Exercises for *Denial*
People who are in denial of their racism are not, by definition, aware of it (or only dimly so). Berating them for this state of affairs is likely to be self-defeating and will drive the denial further underground. Most white people who come on these courses are in denial (arguably every white person is to some extent) but are well intentioned and not obviously hostile to those from BME communities. We, as white people, have, after all, chosen to come on the course. I start by saying that most white people are racist, so we should not be surprised if we find that in ourselves. As I indicated above, I congratulate someone for finding and admitting to a racist thought, difficult to own up to since it feels shaming, but it is the first stage towards doing something about it.

To encourage a discovery of denied racism I may ask people to finish these sentences or something like them with the first thought that comes into their mind, so they do not have time to think of a politically correct answer:

- Black people are…
- White people are…
- When I see a black person I…
- The most impressive black person I have known has…
- I feel…when I see a group of black men.

The result of these and other questions like them can be discussed in pairs and in the group. They can be a starting point for a discussion about hidden racism.

Exercises for *Establishing a new openness and a new equality with the other*
The group leader can ask the group to form pairs and set them any or all of these questions:

- What do you imagine it feels like to be black in today's society?
- Can you remember first seeing a black person and how did you respond?
- How do white people benefit in today's society?
- How do you, in your town, community or family, benefit from the inheritance given to you from people who made their money through slavery and colonisation?
- Can you imagine what it was like to be carried as a slave from Africa to the Caribbean and America? What conditions did they travel in and what happened when they arrived?

If the group is ongoing over several weeks, they could do research in the break between meetings and bring information back. Alternatively, the group leader could provide written information about the history of slavery and colonisation and the genocide of many indigenous peoples for group members to read before the next session. Participants could even use their smartphones or laptops to carry out research on the internet during the meeting, maybe in threes or small groups. They could then discuss what they had learned. Discussions in the group about what has been learned can be very fruitful, provided there is a trusting atmosphere.

Readers of this book might like to set themselves similar tasks and talk to friends about it. Carrying out this exercise myself, I can see that people in my family have specifically benefited from historical processes. On my father's side, there were people who worked in cotton mills in Derbyshire. The cotton will have come from the labour of slaves in America and/or poorly paid workers in India where cotton was imported without tariffs, thus hugely benefiting British industry. Although the owners and managers of the factories would have benefited most, the mills provided my ancestors with a living. Ancestors on my mother's side lived in Southampton, a town which hugely benefited from the slave trade. Although slaves did not come through the port as they did in Bristol and Liverpool, many citizens of Southampton owned slaves and slave ships. The town as a whole would have benefited from this wealth. In the present day, I live in Bath and work in Bristol. Bristol, with Liverpool, was a slave trading town and grew very rich on this trade, as did neighbouring Bath. I benefit by this today, particularly from the wealth of Bath, much of which is currently created by tourists who come to see the beautiful architecture erected on proceeds from the slave trade, which residents benefit from as well, of course.

Exercises for *Guilt and shame*

This aspect can be addressed by the group leader hearing and accepting the guilty feelings that people have and focusing on the issue of guilt both for personal, institutional, national and historic racism. Sometimes it is useful to have a discussion about how far white people should accept responsibility for racism that is not personal to them. Some people feel that we should accept responsibility for forebears and make reparation, and others that we should only accept responsibility insofar as we are still benefiting. It is important to make a space for feelings and thoughts and encourage an open discussion of what arises. However, information about how we still benefit from past privilege may help us to understand the issues more deeply.

Group members could, in pairs or in the whole group, discuss some or all of these questions (or find others):

- In what way do you feel ashamed of your own racism?

- Do you feel ashamed of racist policies of your place of work or your country and what leads you to feel that shame?
- Do you feel ashamed of the racism shown by your countrymen in the past and what leads you to feel that shame?

Exercises for *Owning up to my own white privilege*

Some of the discussion described above informs this aspect of the model. At first sight, it may seem to people that they should not take the blame for historic racism as they were not, as individuals, part of it and were not able to affect it. However, the more it is explored the more people understand that they are still complicit in that they still benefit.

To explore this further here are some more possibilities:

- Repeat the earlier exercise where sentences are finished but this time with more awareness. The group may be asked to 'brainstorm' new sentences.
- Members of the group might also be given the exercise to complete when away from the course. They can be encouraged to notice what they think and feel when they then see a black person. They can be asked to catch the thoughts before these thoughts are dismissed and write them down as soon as possible. This could be discussed in the group if that is possible.
- The group could be given some examples (see Chapter 3) of the 46 ways in which McIntosh (1988) thought she benefited by being white and add some to it.
- Group members may be asked to remember their first sight of a black person or the first time they remember thinking that someone was black. They can be asked, 'What did you think and feel?' and/or 'Did anyone make a comment to you about it?'

Exercise for *Integration*

A state of integration may never be found completely – it may always be something we travel towards rather than something we are able to reach. One indication is the ease with which a white person feels in relating to a black one without the tension of denial. The progress on this road can be discussed in the group if it reconvenes.

Black/white dialogue

If the group is racially mixed, it is not just useful but essential to encourage honest dialogues between black and white members. In order for such encounters to be productive, the group needs to feel very safe so that strong feelings can arise and be contained. The course leader needs to be practised at 'holding' (tolerating and welcoming) strong feelings and, if they are white, to have a good awareness of their own whiteness. Two people running the group, one white and one black, is helpful, particularly if the two have a strong relationship and have been through this process together. White people will need to be at stage 4: *Owning up to my own white privilege*, to really be able to grasp the feelings of black people and how they have been treated by white people during their lives.

The next chapter will explore the dynamics of society and why it is so difficult to lead more socially aware lives as white people, what could help us to change and what might be carried out in a political/societal context to lead to a more peaceful, ecologically sound and racially equal world.

CHAPTER 10

Encouraging Societal Changes in White Awareness

The last chapter explored how individual white people can increase their awareness of their whiteness and white privilege. How can that translate to a wider view of how attitudes need to change societally at regional, national and global levels? Changing one person at a time is likely to be too slow to effect the changes that we need for a more peaceful world, though changes in individuals are also necessary, as we saw in the last chapter. Besides being a good thing in general for society to change, it can also help to find the leadership needed to take societal awareness forward. We start by exploring the disastrous policies that white people have put in place and that are leading us to economic and environmental disaster, along with the difficulty we have in giving up our over-consumption of the world's resources.

Many commentators and authors point out that neoliberalism, a form of capitalism which has been in the ascendant in white countries globally, is beginning to show its internal contradictions and great limitations in bringing real prosperity worldwide (Chomsky, 1999; Savage, 2015; Steger & Roy, 2010; Fioramonti, 2016; Meadows *et al.*, 2004; Piketty, 2014; Wilkinson & Pickett, 2009). Neoliberalism is essentially a white project based in the western world and founded on the wealth that was created through colonial exploitation of other lands and peoples, including the use of slave labour (Piketty, 2014). Amassing wealth by straightforwardly exploiting colonies is clearly no longer possible and the ethical considerations of this are accepted much more widely. In the 19th and early 20th centuries, energy seemed unlimited and there for the taking to power the white, western manufacturing industries which transformed the raw products that were taken from their colonies. Now energy is running out fast. We also know the damage that carbon energy causes our planet. This in turn limits the way in which populations can improve their standard of living (Fioramonti, 2016).

Fioramonti, in his book, *Wellbeing Economy*, says:

> In the age of global economic contraction, there is no way that nations in Asia, Latin America and Africa can develop through the growth economy. These countries don't have the option of colonizing other lands or enslaving other human beings to power their development, like other countries have done before. We are no longer living in the early industrial era, when resources seemed endless and human ingenuity was devoted entirely to subjugating nature and fellow humans for the sake of 'progress'. The World is flat again. Resources have become scarce, and social and political forces have shifted the playing field, reducing the possibility that conventional production will create the billions of opportunities for posterity that the rising middle classes in these continents dream about. (Fioramonti, 2016)

The neoliberal belief that the economy can continue to grow indefinitely is amazingly ubiquitous which, as Fioramonti points out, is illogical in a finite world. It is clear that the over-consumption of the world's resources, the huge increase in global population and the lack of other lands to exploit is leading us to disaster in which nature is likely to set limits to our present lifestyles through climate change and ever scarcer resources.

In their book, *Affluenza* (2014), de Graaf *et al.* show how consumerism has become a disease that makes no one happy, is hard to cure, and has a disastrous effect on the planet. It is a 'virus' which started in America and is now infecting the world. They point out that this disease affects everyone, but in different ways:

> Its symptoms affect the poor as well as the rich, and our two-tiered system (with rich getting richer and poor poorer) punishes the poor twice: they are conditioned to want the good life but given very little possibility of attaining it. Affluenza infects all of us, though in different ways. (de Graaf *et al.*, 2014:5)

They also say, interestingly, that 'If we are to get a handle on affluenza, we must be open to all ideas, not just those deemed "American".' By American, I think we can include 'white'. Neoliberalism has been enthusiastically taken up by all white countries, but it has spread to others as well.

White people have exported the idea that growth in the economy leads to a wealthy society. Fioramonti points out that when South Africa started to be a democratic country led by Nelson Mandela, there was a will to build a country that was fair and equitable for all, so that the injustices of the apartheid era were repaired. Unfortunately, those who had come to power bought into the idea that growth in the economy must come first so that greater equality could be founded on that. 'Growth first' became the watchword (Fioramonti, 2016). Fioramonti explains that Japan, which has not had growth in its economy for over 20 years, actually has a good standard of living. Japanese economists are waking up to the realisation that growth is not necessary for the well-being of the population (Fioramonti, 2016).

So, how can white people, who have exploited the world's populations, caused untold misery, decimated the world's resources so that they are now scarce have exported an economic model that leads to huge inequalities, respond to this situation?

In many ways, this behaviour is like that of an addict – a pathology that is common in the white, western world, particularly America. The authors of *Affluenza* also draw this parallel (de Graaf *et al.*, 2014). Along with our neoliberal economics, we also export addictions. The exporting of addictions is not new. For instance, white colonisers gave alcohol to indigenous people who were then mocked for their drunkenness. The trade in Chinese opium in the 18th century shows up as a particularly shameful episode when the British exported opium into China from India, thus encouraging opium addiction and ensuring that there was a large market. Vast profits were made, and Chinese goods were bought cheaply in large quantities to be sold in Britain. The emperor banned opium and that led to the 'opium wars' which were fought in the mid-19th century to force this trade to continue.

I suggest that, along with private addictions which are prevalent in the West and have been exported over the centuries, the consumerism encouraged by neoliberal capitalism is also something we are addicted to as nations. This addiction to consumer goods is true of whole populations as well as institutions within white western society where the growth economy makes huge profits. Our economies, with their conspicuous and unnecessary consumption, produce spectacular crashes when the excess cannot be sustained. The latest such crash was caused when the banks spectacularly failed in 2008, leading to a depression from which we may never fully recover.

If I am right and this accumulation of consumer goods is addictive, then we must see evidence of addictive behaviour. So, what are the characteristics of addicts? I suggest they are:

- a craving for that which gives temporary satisfaction of the addiction
- increasing tolerance – a need to have an increasing amount of that which feeds the addiction
- a willingness to lie, cheat or steal in order to continue the addictive behaviour – thus overriding personal morality
- denial that the behaviour is a problem
- denial of the extent to which the behaviour is out of control
- denial of the harm done to others because of the addiction.

The addiction may be a substance like drugs, food or alcohol or a less material thing such as work, exercise, gambling, sex or danger (Griffin & Tirrell, 2005). Although these may seem very different from substance abuse, they also have an effect on the body, releasing endorphins and other hormones (Nutt & Nestor, 2013:22) and generating craving.

If we use this as a lens through which to see white, western, neoliberal behaviour, we can explore what this would look like (see below).

A craving for that which gives temporary satisfaction of the addiction

The growth of one's wealth is often addictive in itself, so that it is hard to give up. The growth of one's income has come to be seen as almost a right. We are used to passing on more wealth to our children than was passed on to us. Few people can do that now and many find this very distressing. It is also causing conflict between generations as young people are poorer than their parents were at a similar age.

Increasing tolerance or need to have more of what feeds the addiction

White western people want more and more 'consumer goods'. Something new is often craved and things thrown away before they are worn out. This contributes to another problem that arises from neoliberalism: the mountain of waste that can no longer be found room for and is causing disastrous pollution at sea. Cheap fashion garments are constantly desired and more and cheaper good-quality food is required so that slightly marked or misshapen food is rejected. Cheap holidays abroad are expected, which often include very polluting air flight.

A willingness to lie, cheat or steal in order to continue the addictive behaviour

This is built on past exploitative behaviours, as we saw in Chapter 2. White European nations felt they were justified in greatly exploiting the natural wealth of other countries (their colonies) and appropriating it for themselves. We have grown our economies on the backs of the populations of these countries which has made us very wealthy. Even today, the use of the cheap labour of people from 'developing' economies is exploitative (such as sweat shops in India) and feeds our addiction to inexpensive and plentiful material goods.

Denial that the behaviour is a problem

White people tend to deny that they and their neoliberal project is the core problem in today's world. 'Developing' nations are blamed for pollution while they try to catch up with a white standard of living. Climate change is often denied or downplayed so that policies for controlling it are not accepted and politicians who advocate change are not voted into power. Politicians fear that if they promoted radical policies to stop or reverse climate change or to help those in 'developing' economies, this could spell the death of their political career.

Denial of the extent to which the behaviour is out of control

After the crash of 2008, most western economies found it hard to recover and it seems that we are unlikely to go back to the previous situation of amassing increasing wealth throughout life that we came to take for granted. It is hard for us to take this on board and live within our means, particularly as consumerism is what drives the growth economy. It is hard for us to realise that our behaviour is out of control, even if it has reached a level of excess that spells disaster (Chomsky, 1999).

Denial of the harm done to others because of the addiction

The idea of using economic growth to measure the market value of the goods and services of all nations worldwide does not take into account hidden costs such as the impact on the environment While many white-dominated countries claim to be reducing pollution, in reality we are exporting it elsewhere by exporting our polluting manufacturing bases and then importing the finished goods. The non-white people who do the work often have poor conditions and wages, which means that we can buy the finished goods cheaply in white countries, thereby feeding our addiction (Fioramonti, 2016; Piketty, 2014). A different way of measuring wealth has been suggested. The Genuine Progress Indicator (Wilkinson & Pickett, 2009) takes social and environmental costs into account, not just the production and consumption of goods and services. This alternative model of measuring productivity has not been taken up by any country to date. One country that seems not to have fallen for this addictive neoliberal process is the Himalayan country of Bhutan, where the Gross National Happiness Indicator has been adopted and this includes indicators such as cultural preservation, environmental preservation and good governance as well as economic measures.

Neoliberalism as an addictive process?

So, in the West we are addicted to our neoliberal project – it is an addictive process. We are addicted to consuming the earth's resources – resources which seemed, at the start of the Industrial Revolution, to be infinite and ours for the taking. This included the natural resources of other lands where the people were also seen as our property, over whom we took charge and whom we regarded as hardly human. Having arrived at this state of affairs it is hard for us to give up our addiction, just as an alcoholic or drug addict has difficulty in giving up their habit.

Although those of us who are from the West are no doubt addicted to our personal lifestyle of cheap food and clothing we have grown used to, our addiction is also societal, and it is at a societal level that we must tackle it.

If we can draw this parallel to substance addiction, which is only partly a metaphor – it is also an accurate description of this process – how can we, as a society, be helped to let go of this disastrous habit? There are various 'treatments' for addicts, the best known of which is a 12-step programme, which has been very successful at helping people to give up their addictive behaviour and maintain abstinence. The addict works their way through 12 steps to sobriety and abstinence (Herb, 2004).

The authors of the 12 steps saw taking these steps as a spiritual journey but wrote them in such a way that those who did not believe in God could also use them. They therefore employed the word 'higher power' rather than God. The 'higher power' could be chosen by the person using it, so it could be any power greater than ourselves, including the power of the group (such as an Alcoholics Anonymous group set up to help the addict). I will take each step and then see what this would look like if society came for treatment at an addiction treatment programme.

Here are the 12 steps which addicts are encouraged to take:

- Step 1 – Admit that the addiction is strong, and that the addict is powerless to overcome it alone. We have come to believe that a power greater than ourselves could restore us to sanity.
- Step 2 – Believe that a power greater than the individual could assist with the problem.
- Step 3 – Make a decision to turn life over to a higher power.
- Step 4 – Make an inventory of the self.
- Step 5 – Admit to the higher power and one other person the details of past mistakes and offenses.
- Step 6 – Become ready to remove those defects of character.

- Step 7 – Ask the higher power for help.
- Step 8 – Make a list of everyone the addiction has harmed.
- Step 9 – Make amends to those people, where possible.
- Step 10 – Continue to take an inventory and admit wrongdoing.
- Step 11 – Pray or meditate to understand the will of the higher power.
- Step 12 – Practise the principles and talk about them to other addicts.

So, how would this look if we treat the neoliberal, white, western world as a patient using the 12 steps? I will take one or two at a time:

- Step 1 – Admit that the addiction is strong, and that you are powerless to overcome it alone. We have come to believe that a power greater than ourselves could restore us to sanity.

The first step is very important, maybe the most important. It means giving up the denial that there is a problem and owning that our life is unmanageable, that we are powerless in the face of our addiction. Many addicts think 'I will give up tomorrow', or 'I'll wait until after Christmas' and so on. They may try to give up from time to time and then go back to their old ways.

Taking the parallel of neoliberalism, the kind of behaviour that step 1 would address includes denying that climate change is real, thinking that nuclear power will mean we can go on consuming energy at the present rate, thinking technology will save us, not thinking about where our clothes and food come from and not being prepared to pay what would be a living wage for those who provide us with them. Giving up these things and others would help us to address global inequalities so that the white western world is not consuming most of the world's energy and other resources. Politicians feel discouraged from proposing policies that lead to a cleaner, fairer world as they may well not remain in power if they do so. Parties, such as Green parties, who might advocate these views are very small and it is something of a triumph to have one or two political representatives, who mostly achieve this position by making deals with other parties, for instance by not standing against each other.

- Step 2 – Believe that a power greater than the individual could assist with the problem.
- Step 3 – Make a decision to turn life over to a higher power.

Insofar as addicts are powerless in the face of addiction, they look to a power greater than themselves to help them. The important thing here is to realise that addiction cannot be overcome through willpower alone. If we are to give up our addictive, neoliberal consumerist ways we will have to give up the need to control and allow that something greater is at play here. By using their willpower to give up their addiction, the addict is likely to lose their resolve. It will last for a short time and then they will go back to their old ways. It is only by owning to their powerlessness and allowing the group, or higher power, to help and to take it one day at a time that the addict will be successful. This will lead to the next steps.

- Step 4 – Make an inventory and admit wrongdoing.
- Step 5 – Admit to the higher power and one other person the details of past mistakes and offenses.

Addicts are asked to make a list of the wrongs of which they have been guilty while addicted. In this way, the addict will have to fully face what they have done and how those actions have harmed others. This is often a painful process and takes some time for all the wrongs to be fully owned. It is important that the list is as complete as possible and, having made the list, that the addict admits it to others.

So, our society needs to take a good look at itself, see where the wrongs have been carried out and how these are linked to present wealth. This will include, as has been pointed out above, the past and present exploitation of other lands and peoples in various ways, including colonisation, slavery, poverty wages, discrimination and protectionist policies.

To work at an international level this would have to be a public process similar to a truth and reconciliation process (Tutu, 1998) (which seeks to heal relations between opposing sides by uncovering all pertinent facts, distinguishing truth from lies, and allowing for acknowledgement, appropriate public mourning, forgiveness and healing).

- Step 6 – Become ready to remove those defects of character.
- Step 7 – Ask the higher power for help.

The process of letting go of the idea that we have control of our lives is ongoing and we need to find the humility to realise that we cannot just make a choice to continue but need to allow others to help us.

- Step 8 – Make a list of everyone the addiction has harmed.
- Step 9 – Make amends to those people, where possible.
- Step 10 – Continue to take an inventory and admit wrongdoing.

Having made the list and admitted the wrongs written in it, we are now ready to face up to the people who have been harmed and be determined to make amends where possible. This process may throw up memories of people harmed that have not yet been admitted. The process is painful, and it can seem endless.

Society's exhaustive list of who has been harmed would be a long one. The reader might like to make a list for themselves and go through the other steps as well.

- Step 11 – Pray or meditate to understand the will of the higher power.
- Step 12 – Practise the principles and talk about them to other addicts.

Bill Wilson and Dr Robert Holbrooke Smith, who, with other members of the original group, founded Alcoholics Anonymous and the 12-step programme, were sure that it was only through a spiritual journey that anyone would be able to cope with it. Though many baulk at this, it is helpful to understand that the conscious mind has many ways of deceiving itself and an expectation that addictions can be vanquished through the will mostly ends in failure or in swapping one addiction for another. In the 12-step programme, there is also an important encouragement to help others with this process and live differently in future.

My suggestion to use this 12-step programme for the neoliberal project of the white western world may seem fanciful in the extreme. However, there are elements in it that are necessary, in my view, to ensure that the planet is not plunged into disaster. These disasters include:

- uncontrolled climate change, such as droughts and the melting of the polar ice caps and glaciers, causing a disastrous rise in sea levels

- food shortages leading to mass starvation, making the world unliveable for many people
- violent conflict between those who cling on to wealth and those who become very impoverished
- the threat of nuclear war.

At the very least, the white western world has to face up to the carnage its policies have wrought worldwide and stop denying the problem. This includes no longer making excuses such as suggesting that poorer nations are causing more pollution than western ones. These countries, like India, are often accused of being the greater culprits when it comes to carbon monoxide emissions. This is a dishonest point of view for two reasons. One is that these countries understandably want to achieve the same standard of living as that found in the West and the other, as we saw above, is that the polluting activities of manufacture have been exported to poorer countries where labour is cheap. The goods are then imported back into the West, causing further pollution from the transportation.

This is an example of the way that white people 'use' people from non-white countries. There is a tendency in the West to see 'other' people, such as terrorists, as the biggest global threat rather than climate change. Terrorists who kill people indiscriminately, and the different nation states that sanction them, must bear their share of the responsibility for contributing to a violent and unstable world. However, this occurs in a world where white western culture is arrogantly promoting its neoliberal culture to others, including people to whom western ways are an anathema, and where the West has increased conflict by fighting wars using deadly and sophisticated weapons.

De Graaf *et al.* were brave enough in the book *Affluenza* to say, 'Almost no one dared to mention that anger and envy over the profligate spending of Americans might encourage sympathy for terrorists in developing countries' (de Graaf *et al.*, 2014).

Where morality is concerned, it is important to search one's own conscience before measuring that of others. As it says in the Bible: 'Thou hypocrite, first cast out the beam out of thine own eye; and then shalt thou see clearly to cast out the mote of thy brother's eye.' (Matthew 7:5)

For policies to be put in place that will help to unravel the mess made in the world by white people, we need politicians who are prepared to understand these issues and stand up for them in their constituencies. We need them to show people, in a clear-eyed way, what is really happening in the world. More importantly, we need people to be thoughtful enough to vote for thoughtful and ethical politicians and back them so that the tide will turn to more enlightened and less selfish and self-serving policies.

Maybe we can understand what this would look like by thinking about slavery. Slavery is clearly seen as a bad thing within the western world. Very few would sanction it and people who engage in modern-day slavery are thought of as criminals. This is in great contrast to the time when slave owners were respected members of society. This represents a movement in consciousness that we can celebrate. It is possible for societal attitudes to change so we have some cause for optimism. However, the move we have not made in regard to slavery is to understand the way we still benefit from past exploitation. As I said in Chapter 8, honest and brave dialogue is essential for this move to be made so that societal attitudes do not flip-flop from one position to another and no real forward movement is made.

Conclusion

As a society we, white, western people have become complacent and arrogant in the way we think we know how life should be lived. We like to eat expensive food out of season, often grown cheaply by non-western people, that is flown round the world for our delectation; buy clothes cheaply that are made thousands of miles away, also by non-western people; and recklessly use carbon-based energy that is over-heating the planet. This means we deny the way we are addicted to an unhealthy lifestyle and, like alcoholics, try to encourage others (non-westerners) to join us. This is unsustainable in the long term. My suggestion for doing something about it – treating our society as an addict – may seem far-fetched but, in my view, is serious. Other writers have pointed to the same dynamic, including the authors of *Affluenza* (de Graaf et al., 2014) and *Willful Blindness* (Heffernan, 2011). I have often heard it said that an addict has to reach 'rock bottom' before they feel desperate enough to go for treatment. Let us hope that our white society will not wait until then as that might be too late to avert a disastrous future.

As Alcoff says, 'Rendering our habits visible makes them accessible for reflection and evaluation. This is a possible route for change' (Alcoff, 2015:85).

CHAPTER 11

Consultancy and Training for White Awareness in Organisations

I have explored, so far, how individuals and society can make changes to become more white aware. However, there is one important area that has not thus far been investigated, and that is how white awareness, or the lack of it, is evident in organisations and institutions. Most people are connected to organisations, either through their work or through their religion or through being members of local communities, so this is highly relevant to the life experience of many.

It is well recognised within western societies that organisations can be institutionally racist. Since the UK Metropolitan Police force was found to be so by Sir William Macpherson in the Stephen Lawrence inquiry (Macpherson, 1999), it has become a well-known concept, at least in the UK. Stephen Lawrence was a young black man who was murdered in a brutal racist attack by young white men. This murder was not followed up by police with any enthusiasm and their lack of effort was covered up. There was much call at the time for better police training in racism awareness so that the lack of concern they felt for black citizens should not be repeated. It was after this, in 2003, that an undercover reporter (mentioned in Chapter 3) found that police from the Greater Manchester police force were taught to be 'politically correct' in racism awareness training but retained their deeply racist views (Carter, 2003).

More recently, 19 years after the Stephen Lawrence inquiry, the Bristol

Police were declared institutionally racist by a judge because Bijan Ebrahimi was punched and kicked to death by his neighbour Lee James. Mr Ebrahimi had repeatedly reported constant harassment by neighbours and eventually took photos of them. Rather than arrest the perpetrators, he was arrested himself as a possible paedophile. Books on police racism have been published since the Lawrence report including *Race, Crime and Resistance* (Patel & Tyrer, 2011), and *Are British Police Institutionally Racist?* by Shujaat Husain (2012), a former senior member of the Pakistan police who was arrested for being a conman when he tried to join the British Police. He had been a career police officer with the Karachi police before coming to Britain and was a graduate from the prestigious Massachusetts Institute of Technology (Husain, 2012). Clearly, policies to ensure that institutional racism is no longer found in the British police force have not yet been successful at the time of writing this book.

The same can be said for the American Police Force. The movement, Black Lives Matter, was conceived after the shooting of a young black man by police. In her book about police violence against black women, *Invisible No More*, Andrea Ritchie says:

> As we contemplate the future, there are a number of questions we must ask ourselves, particularly as we enter a period of heightened policing, immigration enforcement, surveillance and militarization, in which manifestations of anti-Black racism, the targeting and exclusion of Muslim and Latinx[4] immigrants, and violations of the sovereignty and spirituality of Indigenous peoples are dramatically increasing. How does centering women's experiences of racial profiling and police violence shape, shift, and expand our understanding of the operation of white supremacy? How does it inform our understanding of gender-based violence and its relationship to state violence? How does it fuel our struggles for reproductive justice? What does it mean for the organizing strategies we employ and the systemic changes we pursue? What are the meanings of and requirements for 'sanctuary' and safety for Black women, Indigenous women, and women of color? Perhaps the greatest challenge of all lies in asking how our reliance on police, prosecution, and

4   Latinx is a gender-neutral term for Latino

prison to prevent and respond to violence has contributed to the experiences of police violence described in these pages, and what it would mean to build structures and strategies beyond police that will produce genuine safety for women of color, especially in hostile terrain. (Ritchie, 2017)

Andrea Ritchie, a woman of colour who can 'pass' as white, recognises here that the problems are systemic within the police and elsewhere and rooted in assumptions of white supremacy.

Various reports of other professions show that the police are not the only institutionally racist profession. In 2014, the UK's Middlesex University published a paper called 'The snowy white peaks of the NHS' which shows that, in spite of a very diverse professional staff, UK National Health Service leadership positions are dominated by white people (Kline, 2014).

Similar findings were published in 2017 in *Equality, Diversity and Racism in the Workplace: A qualitative analysis of the 2015 Race at Work Survey* at the University of Manchester (Ashe & Nazroo, 2017). This shows how stubbornly persistent racist policies and practices at work are in the UK.

Similar studies in the USA, including Princeton University's *Measuring trends in discrimination with field experiment data*, which is a meta-analysis of field experiments and has similar results, show that there is no change in racial discrimination in the hiring of staff over time (Quillian *et al.*, 2017). It seems that shifting racist policies at a governmental level and institutional racism within organisations in both countries are not improving, in spite of attempts to tackle this discrimination with, for instance, anti-discrimination and equal opportunities policies. It is certainly true that organisations are part of wider society and therefore affected by societal attitudes. But change can also go in both directions – from individuals and organisations to the wider society and from wider society to organisations and to individuals – as Wilkinson and Pickett call for in *The Spirit Level*: 'what we need is not one big revolution but a continuous stream of small changes in a consistent direction' (Wilkinson & Pickett, 2009). What follows is a discussion of the way that trainers or consultants can work with organisations to effect changes in their consciousness of race issues and, in particular, white awareness. For those who are not trainers or consultants but work within organisations, the following pages may give some ideas for how their organisation may be helped to change.

So how can organisations, and individuals within them, be helped to become more aware of their whiteness? How can non-white people be more conscious of the way that white awareness fits into a racial discourse within organisations? One way is for the organisation to use an internal or external consultant, coach or trainer to help the organisation reflect on present practices and think about making changes. In order for organisations to change, someone with the necessary seniority must be sufficiently aware of the issues to decide to acquire this training or consultancy. Occasionally, staff at a lower level ask for training and there is enough recognition of the need for this for it to be organised.

If staff in an organisation are concerned enough to want to change its culture regarding racism or white awareness, then it is more effective to make an intervention, with the help of a consultant or trainer, within the organisation itself than send people on external training courses. We find that individuals who have come on courses with a view to changing their own working practice, or to disseminate the learning within the organisation, find it difficult to have an impact and effect any significant changes in the organisation's culture. Organisational cultures are notoriously hard to shift (Kegan & Laskow Lahey, 2009:1) and the individual is likely to become discouraged, particularly if they do not occupy a senior position in the organisation. A senior person such as a human resources director may be more successful after attending a course as they are more likely to be able to effect changes by working with the culture themselves and hand in hand with other members of senior management.

Whether the intervention is one that involves working directly with the organisation or on a separate training course, it is important that it is not merely telling people what to do. Cultural attitudes are not changed that way. Nor is it about telling people what they should think or manipulating them into a 'politically correct' attitude. As can be seen from the example of the police above, this is not a successful strategy for making a difference. Training is much more likely to be effective if there is a genuine dialogue about the issues so that any change is authentic and lasting.

The consultancy/training must be able to change hearts as well as minds. Although information that appeals to our brain's neocortex is useful, it often does not lead to change in underlying attitudes or behaviour (Kegan & Laskow Lahey, 2009:38). Experiential exercises carried out individually, in pairs, in small groups and in a large group (see below), are usually most effective in leading to change, and in the giving and receiving of information and engaging in discussion. Care needs to be taken with how the new thinking gets implemented at work, and follow-up is helpful to make sure that the consultancy/training was not just a tick-box, exercise.

Contracting for consultancy or training

In the Centre for Supervision and Team Development Bath, with whom I work, my colleagues and I have found that the initial contracting is very important when arranging consultancy or training with an organisation. If we are asked to provide consultancy or training for racism or white awareness within an organisation, it is important that the training is for senior-enough people who are in a position to effect a change in culture. More junior staff may be enthusiastic after training, but then become disillusioned as changes in practice are hard for them to put in place.

Naturally, the usual contracting issues need to be attended to such as agreeing fees and other practical matters. However, it is important to establish that all the managers who are commissioning the training, and the staff members who are taking part in it, are clear about the subject and purposes of the consultancy or training. It may be difficult for managers to understand that white awareness is crucial. They may be sceptical about this and prefer a straightforward input on racism awareness. Because of this, the course or consultancy could be about white awareness as such, or white awareness could be part of a course on racism more generally. It may be necessary to give a presentation to explain the approach and negotiate how the subject is tackled.

Organisations often want the training or consultancy to be based at their place of work as this is cheaper and less disruptive. This consideration may trump others, but it is often worth expressing that a neutral, and sometimes more congenial, venue can help staff to relax and be more thoughtful away from the pressures of the job.

If, having successfully completed the contracting stage, you are brought in to help an organisation look at its culture in relation to racism and/or white awareness, then there are various ways in which this can be done, which are not mutually exclusive. You could:

- send out questionnaires to every employee, using an instrument designed for the purpose
- carry out semi-structured interviews with a cross-section of staff which explore each employee's experience of and attitude to race and/or whiteness
- devise a training input for all staff
- devise a series of workshops.

Following the work, the consultant should write a report in which prevalent attitudes within the organisation are laid out. Subsequently, a further input could be put in place to work with staff, helping them to develop their race/white awareness using the exercises described below.

It is sometimes felt that information that arises in the context of training should be completely confidential so that staff are as free as possible to express their views. However, as the organisation, rather than individual staff members, is paying for the work, and is doing so in order for the learning to benefit the organisation as a whole, it is important to find a way to give feedback that does not point the finger at individuals but focuses on feedback of the issues that have arisen on the course. In any case, it is important to be clear about what and how feedback is given so that trust is maintained in the group.

Reviews of the contract

When the contract is set up, it is important to be clear that it can be reviewed at any time, though an agreed time for a review can be decided on as well. This ensures that the contract works well for all parties. Enough time needs to be given for feedback both during and at the end of the course so that issues that arise during the consultancy or training can be addressed at the time.

How the contract is ended

We find that the training input is much more likely to be effective if a good end occurs. A conflictual end in which there is ill feeling, or it simply peters out, will often mean that any learning that did take place in the training is rubbished or ignored.

Dynamics within the group

Any input on racism – whether or not it is white awareness – is likely to raise anxiety. While a certain amount of anxiety is expected and may even be useful, if anxiety is overwhelming, as is shown in Figure 11.1, it is likely to be counter-productive and lead to defensive behaviour and hostile feelings.

Figure 11.1: Learning zones

Learning happens best where there is sufficient discomfort for new learning to be possible and the process does not just confirm a complacent status quo (Hawkins & Shohet, 2012). If the anxiety becomes too much, then learning is inhibited or even rejected. Individuals will vary in how much anxiety they can tolerate and how much learning each is able to bear when anxiety is felt. Some people learn well when they feel a certain amount of anxiety, and others' learning is much reduced if they feel any anxiety at all. It is therefore important for the trainer/consultant to understand that and keep an eye on individuals, reviewing the amount of anxiety that is being experienced and adjusting the work accordingly. It is often sufficient to acknowledge it. That, in itself, can be adequately reassuring for the work to continue at the same intensity.

With the individuals who comprise the training or consultancy group, it is important to be clear about the confidentiality of the group, including when and how information is fed back into the organisation by both participants and consultants/trainers. This needs to be adhered to or re-negotiated if trust in the group and subsequent openness to the learning is to be maintained.

Training groups in white awareness

As well as training for white awareness taking place with specific organisations or professions, it can be carried out in standalone training groups which individuals choose to attend for their own learning. These can be specifically set up for white people on their own or for racially mixed groups. White-only groups can be helpful in that it is easier for people to own up to racist thoughts without non-white people present. As I have shown elsewhere, this may be necessary for racism to be revealed and moved on from. Being accused of racism can be particularly shameful, so it is important for individuals in the training group to feel that they will not be overwhelmingly shamed, or their anxieties raised to a point where learning will be difficult. Exercises that help people to get to know each other first can help, even if they are colleagues who, on the face of it, know each other well.

It is sometimes helpful for participants to form pairs to express their fears and expectations concerning the work of the group, the material being taught and the challenges to come. When the group is ready, I find it is helpful to introduce the notion that we can all have racist thoughts and to recognise that this is more common than we might expect – again this could be discussed in pairs or small groups. When the groups or pairs feed back to the main group I positively acknowledge anyone who has been able to trace and own up to a racist thought. I show the group how important it is to recognise this in oneself, how common it is and that it is an essential precursor to understanding one's own racism.

Having established a training group in which it is okay to be vulnerable and to be open to exploration, I then present the group with some experiential exercises to help them understand their own attitudes, most of which I have laid out in this book. These include:

- finish the sentence exercise (in Chapter 9)
- ten of McIntosh's 46 ways in which she benefited by being white (see Chapter 3)
- the White Awareness Model.

I talk through each of these, especially the White Awareness Model. This includes the importance of understanding the guilt and feeling the shame which arises in order to move through the model. Group members can engage in the exercises that I introduce so that the learning is not only cognitive but is understood emotionally too. True learning only comes when something is known emotionally so that the person is convinced by an 'aha moment' – what Hawkins and Smith call 'transformational learning' (Hawkins & Smith, 2013).

If the group I am working with are all from the same profession or organisation, rather than a mix of people, I will use examples and encourage discussion of the types of issues that arise in their particular situation. If the group is mixed from this point of view, I will encourage participants to explain the contexts in which they work and share these with the group. This often makes for an interesting discussion where similarities and differences in organisational cultures can lead to fresh learning for all.

Mixed training groups

I often say to non-white people that they might be interested to know what the racial environment is like for white people and to hear them struggle with the issue of white privilege. Some non-white people would prefer not to be involved with that, saying it is white people's business to sort that out. Both positions are fair and should be accommodated.

If non-white people are in the group, they can contribute what white privilege feels like for them, which can be helpful, but it is important that white people do not rely on non-white participants to give them information about this as it smacks of the well-known position of black people being the specialists in race. They are often seen as the ones who 'have' a race and therefore know the issues, where white people are neutral and need to have it explained. If non-white people are in the group, it is important to be explicit from the beginning that, within a racial context, we all are en-raced but that white people have been privileged enough not to have noticed it.

The kinds of racial and white awareness issues that arise within organisations

The issues that have already been raised in this book are likely to be evident in work with organisations, including:

- whiteness not being seen as an issue within a racial environment
- a desire to be 'politically correct' rather than to explore racism in depth
- fear of being seen as racist
- hiding racist views, including from ourselves
- not noticing or caring about the diversity within organisations
- worrying about the organisation not being sufficiently diverse
- senior people tending to be white.

Sometimes issues within organisations are 'held' by different people. If there are few non-white people, it tends to be those people who are most aware of these issues and raise them. This can be uncomfortable for them, as if race is an issue for them and not for every other person within the organisation. They may fear being dismissed as having a 'chip on their shoulder'. It is important therefore to ensure that non-white people are not expected to raise issues but that all own them. If this seems to be a persistent issue in the group, then it is probably best to comment on it and let that lead to an exploration.

Working with white awareness is never easy and can be resisted, particularly at first as it may seem like 'political correctness gone mad'! However, staying with it and deepening the conversation without being defensive or aggressive can soon lead the group to understand that this is a serious issue and a significant concern.

Anti-discrimination policy

It has become good practice for organisations to have an anti-discrimination policy to ensure that discriminatory decisions are not made within it. These cover many areas where discrimination is found, including, for example, matters of gender, disability, sexuality, sexual orientation and class, as well as race. It is not often that white privilege is mentioned in such policies regarding race. Many are obviously well intentioned and are clear that people should not be discriminated against because of their race. However, a lack of white awareness is often (or maybe almost always) evident. Take the advice given by the Advisory, Conciliation and Arbitration Service (ACAS), for example:

Employers and employees should be mindful that employees/colleagues will often come from different backgrounds, and aware that there may be cultural differences as a result, particularly regarding customs and values. They should be sensitive and respectful towards such differences. It is good practice for an employer to provide training for staff to establish a culture of respect in this area and provide an understanding of what constitutes acceptable and unacceptable behaviours.

In many respects, this is an admirable statement and should, on the face of it, result in racism not being an issue, both in the experience in the workplace and in the likelihood of any individual getting promotion. If this were true, we would see many more exemplary organisations from this point of view. However, there is a subtle expectation that the 'different backgrounds' mentioned in the statement above are those from non-white countries. The word 'often' used here points to this, as in 'employees/colleagues will often come from different backgrounds'. In fact, difference in background is always present, as are differences in customs and values, whether or not the person is black. Black people being present isn't the only way that difference in culture is an issue in the workplace. I am yet to find a statement of racial equality that mentions white privilege.

Consultants to organisations can challenge this but it may be hard for the organisation to understand the issue if this has not been considered in the past. The exercises mentioned above may help. If the consultancy to the organisation includes work with a group, it could be a useful exercise for the group to try to find a wording for an anti-discrimination policy. They could try to devise an anti-discrimination statement that includes white awareness in it.

For instance, the policy could start like this:

We are aware that, as an organisation, we are mostly racially white and that the proportion of white people is greater than in the population as a whole. The proportion of white people in leadership positions is greater than lower down. White people, as a race, are privileged and this is an example of this privilege. We aim to ensure that this is challenged and that we will work towards guaranteeing a more balanced racial mixture at all levels of the organisation.

For those working with an organisation, it could be profitable for the group, and individuals in the group, to write their own personal statements, share them with others and devise a policy together. This will help people to consider the issues and, if this were being done 'for real' rather than as an exercise, will help them to identify with the statement and have a sense of ownership of it.

This chapter has considered the need for organisations to have anti-discrimination and white-awareness policies and how it is possible to work with organisations to develop these. This will entail helping managers to understand that white people are privileged and assisting them in taking steps to make significant changes. In the next chapter, we will look to the future and what may be in store for white people. The supremacy of the white race is bound to be challenged and how white people respond will be crucial for world peace.

CHAPTER 12

Reparatory Justice

Whether reparations should be made to those wronged by white people and just how they can be made is a hugely contentious issue and one often avoided by governments (McDonald Beckles, 2013). I imagine this is because even considering this idea would reveal something that could be an endless drain on resources and would not be popular with the electorate. After all, the financial benefits accrued by white people at the expense of black people over the centuries have been huge. The general denial and ignorance of the extent of the wrong that has been and is still being perpetrated is so widespread that reparations that genuinely make up for this injustice are likely to be unpopular with the majority of white people. Ta-Nehisi Coates, in writing about the seeming impossibility of Americans facing up to the wrongs committed against blacks, particularly in relation to slavery, seems to feel hopeless about it and says:

> There would be no happy endings, and if there were, they would spring from chance, not from any preordained logic of human morality. I believed this because the reparations claim was so old, so transparently correct, so clearly the only solution, and yet it remained far outside the borders of American politics. To believe anything else was to believe that a robbery spanning generations could somehow be ameliorated while never acknowledging the scope of the crime and never making recompense. And yet that was the thinking that occupied mainstream American politics. (Coates, 2017:159)

The academic, Ana Lucia Araujo, a white Brazilian, now a Canadian citizen, is more optimistic, ironically for the same reason – that it has been on the agenda since the ending of slavery. She has written a book about reparations for slavery (Araujo, 2017), in which she shows how the idea of reparations has been conceptualised since the 19th century and has never been off the agenda. This gives her reason for optimism rather than pessimism about it happening eventually. However, those fighting for it over the years have often been persecuted, such as the imprisonment of those petitioning the United States government in the 1890s when they asked for pensions for slaves. She says:

> Although this context suggests a pessimistic perspective, the debates on reparations for slavery remain very alive. Every year demands of redress continue to be the objects of law suits and Bills and remain present in the public sphere through popular demonstrations, especially when approaching commemorative dates associated with the abolition of slavery. (Araujo, 2017)

So why does Coates say that reparations are 'the only solution'? My own view is that attempts to merely change present practices (such as equality legislation) do not show a real understanding of the depth to which non-white people have suffered in the past and been disadvantaged in the present. It is also unlikely that black people will have any faith in the likelihood of real, meaningful change, unless it is demonstrated by reparations being made. Until or unless, white people fully understand and take on board their privilege, dominance and the exploitation and abuse that black people have suffered as a result, racist attitudes are likely to continue.

There have, nevertheless, been some endeavours to make reparations in a few places. Most of the best attempts that have been made to date could, more properly, be called apologies rather than reparations. These include those made by white people as part of the Truth and Reconciliation process in South Africa (Tutu, 1998). After the apartheid years, those now in power such as Nelson Mandela, with the support of Desmond Tutu, realised that the nation needed to come to terms with the wrongs that were committed and gave the opportunity to those who had carried out atrocities to fully own up to them and apologise to those affected without being punished any other way. This showed enormous magnanimity on their part but also a knowledge that, if something were not done, the country could fall into a violent turmoil which would be hugely destructive to all South Africans, and they thought that white people were needed to keep the economy on track (Deegan, 2011).

Now, 25 years later, whites remain very privileged in South Africa but there is less tolerance of this situation in the black population than there was when black majority rule was instituted under the leadership of Nelson Mandela. Many whites are leaving the country rather than considering these issues and suggesting the paying of reparations. The situation is complicated by there having been a corrupt black president in power from 2009 to 2018, which has apparently not been advantageous to any of the population other than those close to him.

Another detailed and fulsome apology was made by Kevin Rudd, a previous prime minister of Australia (Rudd 2008). He did promise to try to put things right with financial reparations as well as a verbal apology, but many were disappointed in the subsequent actions, which seemed insufficient and did not make much difference to the lives of the First Nations peoples who were supposed to benefit. Since then, in 2017, financial reparations of $75,000 as well as money for funerals are being given to those who were 'stolen generations survivors'. The 'stolen generations' is the name given to indigenous children who were forcefully taken away from their parents and put into homes to become enculturated in white society. This atrocity, which is tantamount to cultural ethnic cleansing, was committed relatively recently. Approximately 1079 children were taken in this way between 1925 and 1969. The reparation scheme will be run for five years. This scheme, though no doubt welcome and just, scratches the surface of the wrongs committed to indigenous people since white people first set foot in Australia.

A white, Australian community psychiatrist, Professor Alan Rosen, has been working hard to redress wrongs perpetrated by mental health providers for First Nations peoples, alongside a growing network of Aboriginal and Torres Strait islander advocates. (Carey *et al.*, 2017). Improving mental health services is important, particularly considering the way that white subjugation and abuse have often led to mental ill health (Rosen, 2018b). This includes transgenerational trauma and post-traumatic stress disorder (PTSD), which are often seen in indigenous people. These could include the trauma of children being forcefully removed from family and community; addictions to drugs and alcohol in people who feel hopeless, and depression if, for instance, they are unable to develop to their full potential, particularly if they are unable to carry out culturally appropriate duties for the community. Suicide among Australian indigenous people was unheard of in their culture until colonisation (Carey *et al.*, 2017) and rare until the 1960s (Rosen & Bridgeson, 2018). It is now much higher than it is in the non-indigenous population.

The Australian First Nations people have been abused and traumatised since white people first arrived in Australia, as have most of the non-white indigenous peoples of the earth. From the earliest years of colonisation, and even in the present day, indigenous Australians have been incarcerated excessively, dislocated from family, traditional community and lands, and admitted to hospital for mental and physical illnesses, more often than the general population, and inappropriately diagnosed and treated (Rosen, 2018b).

Professor Rosen and colleagues have campaigned for respectful and appropriate treatment over decades. He feels that apologies should come from those who are directly connected to the people responsible for the wrongs that were carried out. Mental health professions and their professional organisations, for example, should be the ones to apologise for the way that the mental health system has treated indigenous people historically, and for the continuing harms to this day, that may have been perpetrated or colluded with, whether knowingly or unwittingly (Rosen, 2018a).

Professor Rosen points out that there should be a complete collaboration regarding wording and public commitment to associated actions with those to whom the apology is due: 'to have a chance to be acceptable to a specific indigenous people, they should be consulted while the apology is being developed, and the wording and terms of the apology should be negotiated with them in advance' (Rosen, 2018a).

Carey *et al.* (2017) make the point that an apology should always lead to change and, if it does not, then it will not be respected. The apology by the Australian Psychological Society came after significant collaboration with indigenous people, and the majority of those who drafted the final document were indigenous psychologists. It acknowledged the wisdom developed over thousands of years and that indigenous people themselves should decide what is an appropriate intervention for mentally troubled people. A different way of working was decided on which involved:

- listening more and talking less
- following more and steering less
- advocating more and complying less
- including more and ignoring less
- collaborating more and commanding less (Carey *et al.*, 2017).

Making sufficient and appropriate reparation is fraught with difficulty, particularly if the groups to be compensated have entered the general population, as it has now become hard to quantify how any particular individual has been disadvantaged. The reparation to the 'lost generations' is more straightforward as it is easier to identify the people to whom the reparation should be given and there is a clearly finite number of people who can claim, so the reparation can be realistically costed.

The difficulty of finding a way to give reparations does not mean we should give up on the idea. Not giving reparations, whether or not the reparation is financial, can render apologies meaningless. My husband spoke at a conference about forgiveness some years ago at which one of the speakers, a white South African, illustrated the point and makes the issue very clear. He said that not giving reparations was like apologising to someone for taking their bicycle while refusing to give it back.

Professor Rosen feels that a public apology is not sufficient but can sometimes be a good restart if made with sincerity, in good faith, and if it leads to changes in practices, and an associated public commitment to end the harms and provide much more culturally acceptable policies and services. (Below I show how this might more properly be called 'restitution'.)

Professor Rosen shows that real reparation (the equivalent of giving back the bicycle) might well include changes in attitude, behaviour, government policy and so on. For instance, in America and the UK, a change in policy concerning 'stop and search' where black men would not be unfairly targeted by police, could be *part of* a real apology, and, as I show below, restitution. It is important that it is not just based on following the letter of the law, but on a real desire to change by the people on the ground as well as policy makers. In other words, it would only be sustainable, in reality, if it were carried out with a true intention and not just as political expediency.

Similar work is being carried out in Canada with indigenous people.

The Canadian, Jann Derrick, has spent years trying to understand the world-view of First Nation Canadians (Derrick, 2017). Although she is white, she feels in genuine sympathy with their views. She runs workshops that are designed to address anti-oppressive practice in a way that understands as deeply as possible the underlying issues. The publicity for her workshops says this:

> The teachings and the model have been used globally by professionals seeking to create impactful workshops that address cultural sensitivity, the history of colonization, and supporting critical work to advance anti-oppressive, inclusive practice. The workshop explores the effects of Residential Schools and Canada's Policy of Assimilation and how we can work together to impact meaningful change. (Derrick, 2018)

If this approach became the norm throughout Canada and accepted by the majority of the population, this might lead to First Nations people being fairly treated throughout the country. Could this be called 'reparation'? In fact, this policy would be advantageous for both indigenous and white people. For the white population, the deeply ecological nature of First Nations people, who understand the interconnection of humans to the rest of creation, would be a huge gift and, if white people humbly received that gift, it would be a blessing to all. Although this could be healing, on these grounds, I do not think it could be called reparation. It might, however, be called 'restitution' and be the ground from which white people might understand the *necessity* for reparation in order that we live in a truly equitable way.

My own view is that an apology on its own with only a promise to do better in the future lets white people 'off the hook'. It is not a 'punishment that fits the crime'. Of course, if the punishment did fit the crime, white people would probably have the equivalent of life imprisonment! This is probably unrealistic by any measure and we could argue that 'two wrongs don't make a right'. However, reparations should have some relevance to the crime and should be felt by the perpetrators (including the estates of the perpetrators) and their descendants.

The question of whether reparations should be financial or not seems to me to be crucial. The symbolic nature of money is important. Payment for past wrongs shows the seriousness with which reparations are made. After all, colonisers lived in luxury while the vast majority of colonised people lived in poverty and squalor. However, financial recompense could never make up for what has been lost. Rosen, within his mental health setting with indigenous people, thinks that real, sincere and lasting changes to professional practice and public policy could be a good restart or reboot towards rebuilding trust and hope for justice in relations between indigenous and non-indigenous peoples. He includes in this the necessity for properly appropriate, respectful and evaluated services. It is important that professionals have a deep understanding of the needs of their patients and, where possible, come from the communities that they are serving. Of course, mental health professionals are not in a position to offer financial reparation but can change professional practice. As we saw above, Rosen importantly says that those to whom reparations are given should be included in any discussions about the nature of the reparations. I have not seen this articulated anywhere else but it seems an obvious strategy for getting it right.

In the same way that I think a step-by-step process is needed in order for white people to become thoroughly aware of their whiteness, and what it means in terms of their privilege and dominance, so I think a process is needed that takes white people towards being able to give reparation and understand the necessity for it. It is important that reparation is given ungrudgingly and with a full understanding of what needs repairing and why. Figure 12.1 shows the steps that need to be taken.

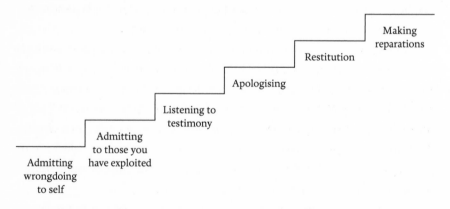

Figure 12.1: Steps towards reparation

These steps show that an apology is based on acknowledging and taking on board the wrongs that have been perpetrated. This apology can then lead to restitution, which can then lead to full reparation. Each of the steps in this process is explored below.

Admitting wrongdoing to self

This comes with the first step beyond Denial on the White Awareness Model when the white person can see that a wrong has been committed that is not merely in the past – black people still suffer, and white people still benefit. When that acknowledgement is fully present it takes us to the next stage.

Admitting to those you have exploited

This involves being able to fully admit our own fault, not just to other white people but also to black people. This admittance can lead to the next step.

Listening to testimony

This stage might also come before the *Admitting wrongdoing to self* step, but I have put it here as it might be that white people can only listen well when they have become more open to hearing it. This was the case in the Inquiry into the Grenfell Tower fire – a London tower block of apartments that burnt down because of flammable cladding on its outside walls. The tower block provided social housing and many of the tenants who died were not white. When the Inquiry into the cause of the fire was first set up there were many protests about who would hear the the evidence. Many of the residents thought that people who would hear it were not sufficiently in touch with the impoverished and ethnically diverse community who lived in the block. This was rectified by the addition of two more judges. It was then decided that the Inquiry would start by hearing the testimony of survivors. This was very powerful and put their experiences in the centre of the context of the failings of local government and contractors to ensure that the tower was safe. Listening to testimony is important both for those who have been wronged in order to ensure they feel heard and for those who have perpetrated the wrong to ensure that they hear and accept their responsibility.

Apologising

Apologies need to be clearly genuine and also specific. An apology that merely says, 'I apologise for our exploitation of black people' does not go far enough and does not demonstrate a full knowledge of the wrongs that have been committed. Tony Blair expressed 'deep sorrow' in an attempt at an apology for slavery in 2007 which did not go far enough as it did not recognise any fault. The Australian Prime Minister, Kevin Rudd, gave a much more fulsome and detailed apology in 2008. David Cameron (the then British Prime Minister) was again urged to apologise when he visited Jamaica in 2015 but he failed to agree to this. Apologies are a good start but, even with a small amount of money given with them as reparation, are not enough in themselves, and certainly are not successful if responsibility is not taken for the wrongs inflicted.

Restitution

Restitution may be sufficient in some circumstances as with the restitution of good public services (see above). I am using this word to mean 'making amends by ensuring fair and equitable practices for all members of the population'. Making present-day practices and services equal for all people within society is restoring a situation which is fair and just. It does not make up for the past, unless it partially does so by actually helping people to overcome the disadvantage that past practices have led to. If this were to have any credence it would probably need to be carried out by mostly black/indigenous professionals and with public money.

Making reparations

By 'reparation', I mean owning up to liability for past wrongs and taking realistic steps, not only to correct them, but to make up for them. How to achieve this in a way which is genuinely fair would be a difficult task, but, if it were approached with a good heart, might go a significant way to healing the wrongs of the past.

These steps could be uncovered and identified as part of the process towards white awareness discussed in Chapter 9. Figure 12.2 shows what the White Awareness Model would look with these added.

Having indicated that white people need to make the shift in consciousness that I have been advocating in this book, it may seem that I feel, like Coates, pessimistic about the possibility that meaningful reparations might be made, particularly because of the huge steps that white people need to take. I think it is unlikely that significant measures will be put in place in the near future, but, like Rosen's contributions mentioned above, smaller but very significant steps could be made where there are people of good will to ensure that it happens. So what else could be done if there *were* sufficient good intentions? What now follows are some thoughts that I have had about what *listening to testimony*, *restitutional* and *reparational* measures could be achieved in the near future if there *was* good intent.

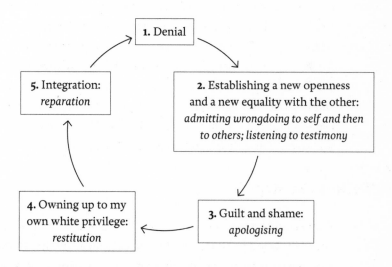

Figure 12.2: Steps towards making reparations mapped onto the White Awareness Model

'Listening to testimony' steps

- Towns all over the world, including Liverpool, Bristol, Southampton and London in the UK, already have slavery museums that show ways in which the slave trade has benefited the population. Slavery museums are also found in other countries which used slaves, including America. The Wright Museum of African American History has a replica of a slave ship, which is a powerful reminder of that shameful history and could be copied elsewhere. These museums could extend their brief to show how the town is still benefiting. Further museums could open and help to ensure that every school child from the age of 7 knows in detail how slaves suffered. Museums of this sort can help move people out of the denial stage of the White Awareness Model and start the cycle to the *establishing a new openness and a new equality with the other* stage. It is a *listening to testimony* step in the *steps towards reparation* that can help people to understand the next steps of *restitution* and *reparation*.

- The UK National Trust and other owners of historic houses in western countries could be clear about the slavery that is part of the history of the house, showing how and where slaves lived, how they got there, what they ate, what their tasks were, the numbers of hours they worked and what happened to them after the emancipation of slaves. This could be embedded among all the information being given out to visitors, but they could also have certain weeks in the year which are especially about slaves, with activities for children, special exhibitions and so on. This is also a *listening to testimony* step.

'Restitution' steps

- There could be free special educational classes for adults (maybe this could include any educationally disadvantaged adults) to help them increase their chances of making a good living. For some black people in poor communities, drug dealing seems to be the only way of funding a life that is not very impoverished (Thomas, 2017). Research carried out by Agata Vitale and myself showed how refugees consider the lack of meaningful work as the main cause of mental ill health. Government money to provide free courses which prepare people properly for work would go a long way to help. An intervention following our research in Bristol, UK, includes the provision of free mentoring and internships from willing companies (Vitale & Ryde, 2016). This is *restitution* in that it makes an unfair system fair for black people.

- The criminal justice system could take into account the difficulty some people from black communities have in taking a full part in wider society. This includes poverty, lack of good education and racism. Past and present ill-treatment has contributed to present-day criminality, such as knife crime among gangs, and drug dealing. Much more public money could be given to help young black people live more fulfilling lives and show that they have a stake in society and society has a stake in them.
- Companies could be made to ensure that no slaves or people on poverty wages are in the supply chain of goods.

'Reparation' steps

- Government 'aid' could be increased, renamed and re-imagined as reparation. This would give a different dynamic to what is, at present, rather patronising. Instead of handouts to countries that need 'help' because they are thought not able to help themselves, this would be paid in recognition of the way that western countries have contributed to their present situation. This situation includes taking wealth from the country, taking people into slavery and other actions such as drawing inappropriate boundaries and privileging one tribe over another, thus causing unnecessary conflict.
- Members of individual families who have historically directly benefited by the slave trade could put money into a fund to help disadvantaged non-white groups.

These suggestions fall a long way short of full reparations, but they start to make smaller steps which can lead the way. Perhaps the reader could think of more practical steps that could be taken.

164 WHITE PRIVILEGE UNMASKED

Reparation is a difficult area for white people to contemplate as it means giving up their privilege and owning and taking responsibility for past wrongs. Many people I have spoken to see it as unjust for white people to feel responsible for sins committed in the past but, as we have seen throughout this book, black and non-white people are still disadvantaged, and white people are still benefiting from past exploitation. If this running sore in society is not seriously addressed, it will continue to be an injustice from which we all suffer.

As in other places in this book, I have suggested a process towards making reparations which I believe is more helpful and realistic than simply urging that reparations should be made. It has been shown, in Northern Ireland, for instance, that a *process* towards peace is more likely to be successful than simply asserting that peace should be made. Of course, this is immensely difficult and usually not entirely successful but, if we are to try to ensure that the majority of the population buy into the project, we need to have a process that speaks to all and takes as many people as possible towards this difficult task.

So, what after reparation has been made? Maybe that could be the final realisation of Martin Luther King Jr's Dream when the 'sons of former slaves and the sons of former slave owners will be able to sit down together at the table of brotherhood' (King, 1999). Professor Rosen suggested a seventh step of 'Working towards transformation' (Rosen, 2018a). Reparation will set the scene for that to become a reality, but it will still need work to constantly build and rebuild trust until race is no longer an issue, just a faint memory read about in history books. Children will scratch their heads and wonder how people could have thought that the colour of someone's skin had any meaningful significance.

CHAPTER 13

Where Next for White People?

It has been suggested (Alcoff, 2015; Jacques, 2012; Luce, 2017; Wilkinson & Pickett, 2009) that the dominance of white people and their neoliberal hegemony is likely to fail in coming years, either gradually or suddenly. Other nations such as China, India and Russia are becoming more prominent economically and politically and more assertive globally. China, for instance, is set to overtake America in the size of its economy by 2025 (Jacques, 2012:3) and is reversing decades, if not centuries, of withdrawal from international activity and making an impact on the global stage. An example of this is China offering aid and infrastructure projects to African nations (Rotberg, 2009), fulfilling contracts in various other parts of the world such as the Middle East and South America (Jacques, 2012). China truly makes its influence felt in this way, while also being a major exporter of goods.

This kind of threat to western dominance causes a sense of panic among some white people and nations and may, at least partly, account for the rise of right-wing parties in the past few years, while the political discourse emphasises retrenchment to 'traditional values' and national pride. White people have convinced themselves so strongly, and over such a long time-span, that their ways are superior to those of other cultures, that they find it hard to imagine that any good could come out of a country that espouses different philosophies. This is apparently in spite of the fact that from a non-western perspective many western values and cultural habits deserve to be criticised as self-centred and materialistic from a principled standpoint. Other nations feel threatened by western economic philosophy and practice, and the potential military threat rich nations can wield. As Luce (2017: 106) says in his book, *The Retreat of Western Liberalism*, it is tempting to imagine that the whole world craves to be western. But he says, 'We can no longer have any confidence in that. It was remarkably arrogant to believe the rest of the world would passively adopt our script.' However, it is hard to give up deeply held and cherished beliefs. Heffernan makes this point convincingly in her book, *Willful Blindness*:

> Our most cherished beliefs are a vital and central part of who we are – in our own eyes and the eyes of our friends and colleagues. Anything or anyone that threatens that sense of self produces pain that feels just as dangerous and unpleasant as hunger or thirst. A challenge to our big ideas feels life-threatening. (Heffernan, 2011)

This is true, not only of individuals, but of groups – and the pressure to maintain our beliefs can be even stronger in groups where it is not only important to be faithful to our individual principles but also to remain faithful to a group with whom these views are held in common (Heffernan, 2011). Our sense of ourselves as individuals and as members of communities and cultures is maintained by emphasising similarities between 'us' and seeing those who are different as 'them'.

If there is a threat to white dominance – which seems credible at this time – how could it happen and what are the likely scenarios that may play out? I will point to and comment on a few possible ones, starting with the most destructive ones, and proceed to the most optimistic.

1. All-out war

By the time you read this book, Donald Trump may not be the President of the USA. However, as things stand at the time of writing, he is, and if his tweets are anything to go by, he could easily start a war. When he is not the President, this scenario may be just as likely or only slightly less likely. Western powers consistently maintain that they are the only ones who can be trusted with nuclear weapons. What I perceive in this stance, and deeply held conviction, is that it implies that 'letting' other nations have nuclear weapons is like giving a gun to a child. The word 'letting' here implies that western countries, or more specifically, America, have the power to say whether or not any particular country can have nuclear weapons. In the past, when America and the West were conducting the Cold War with the Soviet Union, it was an unwritten rule that they would act as if they would use nuclear weapons but would not take this final step. In that way, a balance was struck which kept war at bay. These rules no longer seem so clear and the threat from Kim Jong-un, the leader of North Korea, who is also a seemingly unpredictable leader, is not insubstantial. It would force other nations to take sides and join in. Terrible though this option is, it cannot be discounted.

My own view is that no country can be trusted with nuclear weapons and they should all be multilaterally disarmed.

2. Ecological meltdown

If we are to continue to use the world's resources at the rate and in the way we are presently doing, and growing our populations at the same exponential rate, we are likely to see unsustainable climate change in which millions will die and the present-day infrastructures, such as energy, water, transportation and so on, will no longer be viable. The present globalised world will become unrecognisable. With global warming, sea levels will rise and the shape of our coastline will completely change, leaving many cities under water, including most of our biggest conurbations which are near the coast, such as New York, Washington, Sydney, London, Beijing and Rio do Janeiro. Governments will struggle to survive, and the rule of law and order may well break down. No doubt pockets of human beings will survive and may learn to live in greater harmony with nature. In their book, *Limits to Growth*, Meadows *et al.* (2004) show how, without giving up the 'growth economy' and attending to ecological necessities, there is likely to be a 'collapse' of the human footprint along with increased mortality and rapid decline in consumption. In other words, if we do not do this reduction of consumption ourselves in a controlled way it will be forced on us by natural processes which will be activated by over-consumption of the world's resources and pollution of the earth, air and seas.

It is possible that this scenario may occur after, or as a result of, one of the other disasters. In order to minimise the risk of this scenario, we need to be acting with a lot more urgency than we are at present, and I have shown in previous chapters how the white, western world is the most culpable for bringing us to this situation and therefore needs to be most proactive in making changes.

3. Other military options

In recent years smaller, more localised wars have been prosecuted by western countries, mostly to try to depose leaders of countries of whom, often for good reasons, the West disapproves. Often these leaders employed tactics which were clearly destructive to their own people. Saddam Hussein, for instance, used gas against the Iraqi Kurds, but the effect of the war on the people of the countries involved was often worse than the action taken by those leaders, causing untold 'collateral damage' and reducing significant parts of the country to rubble. This is obviously and inexcusably the case in Iraq, Afghanistan and Syria.

Some of these wars will, no doubt, be 'proxy wars' where the antagonists are backed by another country which is furthering its own interests by encouraging the war. It often helps one of the parties by providing weapons and other material assistance. We may well see further proxy wars in the future when powerful nations want to further their own ends with minimal risk.

These wars have also been fought in a vain attempt to contain terrorist groups. It seems that terrorism as an ideology cannot be destroyed by military intervention and, in fact, can be fuelled by such wars, driving potentially more moderate people into the arms of extremists, strengthening their force beyond expectation and intention – essentially by deepening the polarisation between 'them' and 'us'. This 'war on terror' is particularly harmful to minorities, women and children. But most dangerously, these wars have alienated Middle Eastern peoples and deepened the divide between Islamic populations and western Christian countries.

Finding good ways to act under these circumstances presents all of us with complex and difficult questions. When well-intentioned westerners see the suffering of people arising from dictatorship and extremist groups, often the call for a military response is heard in an attempt to bring an end to that suffering. Unfortunately, such interventions tend to increase the torment people in war zones suffer. Recently, such military interventions have resulted in huge numbers of refugees making perilous journeys to Europe. Those who make it to the West mostly live in poverty, with shaky legal status, and face racial discrimination. The suffering which arises from military intervention is immense, since to apply this policy in a country with a different culture is always problematic. It is hard to understand the historically determined political complexity of countries that are different to one's own. This cannot really be understood from an outsider's perspective and will generate a host of unintended consequences. Of course, abusive leaders and extremist groups are also guilty, but this does not mean that the West is absolved from guilt. Nobody is let off the hook. Everybody is accountable for their own actions. We must not make the mistake of simply blaming others but must investigate and remedy our own irresponsible and unethical actions, which contain the seeds for further polarisation and conflict.

Bearing this context in mind, a second future scenario is that similar wars continue, leading to greater and greater terrorist threats in the West. This will have two effects:

- Many other very serious attacks may occur such as in 9/11, which will harden attitudes against Islamic people.
- Attacks could be committed in cyberspace and could create even more mayhem than a physical attack by shutting down essential services like electricity.

These attacks could destabilise western economies and make them vulnerable to collapse. Greater conflict on our streets and in our communities could reach a tipping point of ungovernable violence. If services such as water and electricity do not function, it will not take long before life as we know it becomes untenable.

4. Power blocks

President Putin is clearly determined to see Russia providing a counterweight to American power and global interventionism. He has suggested that there should be several power blocks in the world, all of whom have their own cultural ways of acting and do not interfere with each other's policies with regard to the populations within their own spheres of influence. Certain nations such as Russia, India, China and America would be the power brokers in their own global regions. If this policy were put in place throughout the world, possibly through the United Nations, though maybe just by default, this would mean that other countries could not be appealed to if leaders were undemocratic or totalitarian and indulge in human rights abuses. This is a particular fear in regard to Russia, which seems, on the face of it, to be prepared to attack individuals in other countries with chemical or radioactive weapons, quite apart from claiming power over countries like the Ukraine because they were part of their previous sphere of influence. It does seem that, in the West, we tend to have an assumption that other countries, left to their own devices, will be harmful to their own people and that white westerners are the only ones who can do something about it. Nevertheless, smaller nations might suffer under this dispensation, so this scenario is not ideal but may be preferable to the two above.

In his book, *The Dawn of Eurasia*, Bruno Maçães (2018) sees Europe and Asia becoming one super continent with no one country dominating. He points out that Asian countries have fewer similarities to each other than Europeans who have been able to make common cause and form a more unified power block. Maçães's research took him on a six-month tour of areas bordering Europe and Asia and led him to predict that the world will be dominated by China, Japan and India plus a fourth power which he is not so certain about but interestingly includes Germany. He plumps for Indonesia as the most likely fourth option. Maçães is not so clear about whether these countries will dominate by making spheres of influence. He envisages something more fluid and less planned than Putin's vision. He says: 'It is increasingly a composite world – as Eurasia itself is composite word – where very different visions of political order are intermixed and forced to live together' (Maçães, 2018).

5. The status quo + learning

I have added '+ learning' to the title of this scenario as I think that having an option called 'The status quo' without the learning is probably not an option that is likely to be sustainable for more than a few years. Given stable and pragmatic leadership with good diplomatic skills, it is possible that we may continue for many decades as we are at present – if certain lessons are learned. These lessons concern western nations clarifying what kinds of intervention are really helpful when other countries are under threat from their leaders or insurgent groups. An ability to work with other countries that become increasingly powerful like China and India in a co-operative and culturally educated and sensitive way is bound to be in the best interest of all. All participants in such transnational dialogue must feel that everybody's interests will be served. Making proportionate space for non-western powers does not have to necessarily mean a threat to western ways, particularly if western people are willing to learn from such dialogues, rather than using them to proselytise western culture. Western democracies, whose people and governments are concerned about human rights abuses elsewhere, may become more skilled in tackling these diplomatically and without humiliating their partners in dialogue.

6. More radical change towards equality

As advocated by socialists within the West and by the authors of *The Spirit Level* (Wilkinson & Pickett, 2009), a turn to a more equal society than that afforded in the present dispensations, particularly by neoliberalism, could also mean that white westerners are more prepared not to dominate worldwide but to live with more justice and equality than they do at present. It is often assumed by those in the West that we have just and democratic societies. In fact, this is far from the truth. Consider, for example, huge multinational organisations wielding more power than governments and producing a few mega-rich people who do very well – while others, often now called the 'precariat' (Savage, 2015:20), live below the poverty line. Large multinational corporations have recently been found to create sway over the electorate through targeted mass marketing based on stolen personal data. Making changes which reverse societal inequality would involve a huge cultural transformation, and as Wilkinson and Pickett demonstrate (2009), it would also generate huge benefits, not just to those at the bottom of our very unequal society, but those at every other level, too. They show very convincingly that every measure of social well-being – such as physical and mental health, obesity, life expectancy, crime, violence – is improved for the whole population if society is more equal. This is also true of good race relations. They say, for instance:

> The ethnic divide increases prejudice and so widens income differences. The result is that both communities suffer. Rather than whites enjoying greater privileges resulting from a larger and less well-paid black community, the consequence is that life expectancy is shorter among both black and white populations. (Wilkinson & Pickett, 2009:2525)

So, it is clear that white populations insisting on their own dominance in order to prosper are making an incorrect assumption. Research shows that it would serve all of us well to be on an equal footing. These authors also suggest that 'human group conflict and oppression, such as racism and sexism, stem from the way in which inequality gives rise to individual and institutional discrimination' (Wilkinson & Pickett, 2009). If it does become clear that greater equality delivers greater peace, prosperity, health and general happiness to all, then hanging on to the ideology of white dominance may gradually not seem so important – but it is an assumption so deeply ingrained that it cannot be easily shifted.

The future is very uncertain and white supremacy and the attendant privilege may well be a thing of the past. Our privilege is not just a matter of economic dominance, its domination is built on a powerful and taken-for-granted assumption that white ways are the only ones which can create a peaceful and prosperous world. Losing economic dominance may well have a knock-on effect of losing our ascendency and this is bound to make a difference to white people's cultural hegemony as well. With economic supremacy comes power and influence globally. White people seem to be in the process of emotionally withdrawing to their own countries and trying to find the old certainties. However, these countries themselves are now very multicultural and this could become an exciting time of cultural transition. White people could become less arrogant, own their privilege and be prepared to take part as genuinely equal partners within the international community. Issues of indisputable importance such as climate change, environmental degradation and threats from nuclear energy could be seriously tackled.

Nation states could become less important, with their need to be self-interested at the expense of others, and war could be thought of as an aberration that needs containing rather than an acceptable response to being threatened by evil monsters.

To achieve this, human beings must become less attached to their narrow self-interests and understand that the earth is one complete body with all living and inanimate objects parts of the whole. What hurts one hurts all, just as an injury to one part of our body causes the whole to suffer. Everybody fits within their own niche in the greater whole so, if one part is advantaged, it leads to a distortion in the whole system which benefits no one in the long run, even if it seems to at first. As the rapper Tupac Shakur says: 'Thug Life', which is an acronym for 'The Hate U Give Little Infants Fucks Everyone.' I learned that from Angie Thomas's wonderful book *The Hate U Give* (2017) which is about a young girl who witnesses the killing of her friend by a policeman.

How will we achieve an ability to live in this way? It will need leadership from many – not one heroic leader. Enlightened leaders can help if they do not work alone but individual leaders can become despotic or idealised, which often leads to disillusionment. They tend to get replaced by ones who promise 'more' but then cannot really deliver what they promise. The way to a more peaceful world will mean some have to do with less than they have been used to, in our less equal world. At present, America is much wealthier than other countries though its economy is growing less rapidly and the difference between rich and poor is great (Deaton, 2013; Piketty, 2014). Many of the poor are black. This is a hard road and a painful process but necessary if we are to survive the environmental and political crises that loom ahead of us. Let us hope that we are able to achieve it for the sake of our children, grandchildren and great-grandchildren.

In the last chapter, we will explore further what is needed for this change to come about.

CHAPTER 14

And Now Towards the Needs of the Future

I will now bring the ideas of the book together and consider the pressing necessities we need to consider for the future. How might we respond to the challenges that are coming over the horizon? In a fast-changing world, we can never rest on our laurels since the future is bound to bring fresh challenges.

We have seen how white privilege has been built on a history of white people creating race differentiation and hierarchisation between races. This created the arrogant and ignorant belief in white supremacy over a long period of colonial exploitation and since those colonies were disbanded. It has led to over-consumption in the West and great inequality and suffering worldwide. This pattern of western dominance is finally in crisis. I have gone into some detail about how this situation arose, what the privilege of being white consists of, its effects on the world in general and how we might approach doing something about it, as individuals, as institutions and as nation states. In Chapter 12, I also outlined some possible future scenarios.

To end, I want to look in more detail at what it will take for us to become more able to make the necessary changes in our ways of being in the world. I will explore what makes it so difficult for us to bring about the changes which are urgently required if we are to live in a fairer world with more equal chances for all communities in our societies to flourish. I will clarify and crystallise some of the ways in which we blind ourselves to the privilege that being white conveys to white people.

In her book, *Willful Blindness*, Heffernan (2011) shows how, as human beings, we tend to hide from unpalatable truths, particularly if they threaten our sense of self or are too painful to be taken on board. She shows how denying knowledge of difficult truths harms others and that we are still responsible for the consequences of this refusal to declare the truth. She asserts that this is true morally, just as it is the case in a court of law where it would constitute withholding of known evidence. She gives many examples in which she shows how people – to comply with authority or because it threatens our own interests – have not acknowledged the truth, stood up for it and thus failed to take responsibility for their potential contribution to justice. She cites other examples where people have been witnesses to truth and have declared it, even when it was not in their interest that it come out – some people have been willing to face being penalised for standing up for truth.

In the case of being white, it is easy for us white people to 'not know' the harm that has been done in our name in the history of colonisation and slavery – and that repression and exploitation of vulnerable people is still happening in many different guises. The privilege that falls to us as white people persists. It behoves us then to face the truth and the cold wind of recognition and acknowledgment which blows away illusions, denial and pious lies. Heffernan also shows how, as human beings, we show a marked preference for 'people like us' even when rationally we hold that we prefer to enjoy diversity (Heffernan, 2011). This provides a context for understanding that white people prefer to be with other white people. Some effort is required to move beyond that bias and accept the work entailed in understanding those who do not fit into our in-group. In the light of this, nothing excuses willful blindness to historically accrued injustice.

So what privileges do we tend to be blind to as white people? As an exercise in facing up to this and as a way of summing up what we have discovered in this book, I have thought of eight ways in which white people maintain their privilege. Maybe the reader can think of more.

1. In recent centuries, white people have been globally dominant and therefore, without thinking about it, feel a historical certainty that they are the dominant race.
2. Their certainty about this has led them in recent decades to assume that, within a racial context, they are racially neutral. Others 'have a race'. As Dyer says, 'There is nothing so powerful than being "just" human' (1997:2).

3. Not having to think about race leaves energy for thinking about other things.

4. Artefacts and evidence of your forebears' activities are all around us – we take this built environment for granted, leaving its origins unquestioned. We feel rooted in our environment. This is even true for white people visiting other countries that have been colonised by white people where white architecture and other artefacts like street furniture are in evidence, but are populated, at least in part, by non-white people whose ancestors did not build these things. South Africa, Canada, Australia, America and India are examples of colonial cultural take-over.

5. Living in a country of ex-colonisers, such as the UK and some European countries, or in a place which used slave labour, like the USA, then we must acknowledge that the wealth created in the past has been built on the exploitation of non-white people for centuries, right up to the present day. It still makes ex-colonising countries much wealthier than they would have been without that history and practice of exploitation.

6. Within European countries, the cultural habits, behaviours and practices have been developed by white people over centuries. This gives a sense of deep-rooted cultural placing, membership and belonging – a world we take for granted, which gives us security.

7. If your ancestors were slaves, then your surname will have been given to you by slave owners and not by your families according to ancestral custom. This is not true of white people, whose ancestors passed their names to the following generations. This gives a sense of being founded and rooted in a known and secure history, not one in which there was extreme suffering, alienation and cultural deprivation.

8. Much of the art, literature, music and so on that is mainstream in the culture is white. Although non-white people's cultural richness is becoming more mainstream, it is still on the fringes, which gives the individual a sense of being on the margins of society.

These are things to which white people may well be wilfully blind. But there is another matter that we might be reluctant to see. This concerns not so much issues of privilege, but that we are being confronted with the fact that white people and western societies are losing their hegemonic dominance in the world.

As we saw above, the world is changing fast, which contributes to right-wing governments and politicians gaining ground in today's world. The policies advocated by right-wing groups tend to look for the familiar, to fear diversity and reassure people that change can be kept at bay. Those 'not like us' should be 'sent back to where they came from'. Our privileged place is being challenged even now. The tendency to think that white, westerners' ways are the only right and successful ones is deeply challenged now. History is full of empires that arise and fall, so it is unlikely that western neoliberalism will last forever and there are signs that it is weakening fast. With China and other Far Eastern countries becoming more powerful, they will gain ascendancy and increasingly challenge white, western dominance. In his book, *When China Rules the World*, Martin Jacques points out:

> There has been an assumption by the Western mainstream that there is only one way of being modern, namely by adopting Western-style institutions, values, customs and beliefs, such as the rule of law, the free market and democratic norms. This, one might add, is an attitude typically held by peoples and cultures who regard themselves as more developed and more 'civilized' than others: that progress for those who are lower down on the developmental scale involves them becoming more like those who are higher up. (Jacques, 2012:13)

This point of view is becoming less tenable as our economies become less dominant and our societies less successful. In *The Future of Whiteness*, Alcoff says:

> White identity has not had to share much of anything. It has been inculcated with a vanguardist illusion for over a century that has configured European whites as the scientific, technological, moral, artistic and political leaders of the human race. (Alcoff, 2015:24)

And:

> Whiteness will no longer be invisible when the majority of Americans find it so very visible in its foregrounded status as the newest minority. It will no longer be the default identity of leadership nor will it be able to justify its cultural hegemony. (Alcoff, 2015:25)

This may seem like a fearful future for white people and we may be anxious about the possibility that there will be some retaliation for the way we have treated non-white people in the past or, indeed, that a natural process of being in a one-down position will mean that we might be discriminated against in the way we discriminated against others. One thing is clear, it would be hard to justify an assertion that western neoliberal democracy has delivered peace, security, equality and freedom from poverty for all, so that another dispensation will be bound to be worse if it does not aspire to our values.

As Wilkinson and Pickett (2009) say, working towards equality is the surest way to improve the well-being of all members of society whoever they are. This is far more important than trying to hang on to our dominance and privilege, whatever befalls us in the future. It would certainly be a better legacy to leave for the world, if and when we lose our attachment to dominance and privilege as white people. Martin Luther King (and quoted by Barack Obama) said, in his wisdom: 'The arc of the moral universe is long, but it bends towards justice' (Rieder, 2013). In saying this he was précising an American Unitarian minister, Theodore Parker, who was born in 1830 and was a tireless worker towards the abolition of slavery. In a sermon, he said:

> Look at the facts of the world. You see a continual and progressive triumph of the right. I do not pretend to understand the moral universe, the arc is a long one, my eye reaches but little ways. I cannot calculate the curve and complete the figure by the experience of sight; I can divine it by conscience. But from what I see I am sure it bends towards justice. (May, 2013:100)

Let us hope that this is correct and that more of us will join those actively working to that end.

References

Aanerud, R. (1997). 'Fictions of Whiteness: Speaking the Names of Whiteness.' In R. Frankenberg (ed.) *Displacing Whiteness*. Durham and London: Duke University Press.

Abram, D. (1996). *The Spell of the Sensuous*. New York, NY: Vintage.

Advisory, Conciliation and Arbitration Service (ACAS) (n.d.). Retrieved from www.acas.org.uk/index.aspx?articleid=1849, accessed on 26 September 2018.

Akala. (2016). My Thoughts on the EU Referendum. Retrieved from http://illastate.posthaven.com, accessed on 26 September 2018.

Alcoff, L. M. (2015). *The Future of Whiteness*. Cambridge: Polity Press.

Amnesty International (2018). End Inhumane Overuse of Detention Now. Retrieved from www.amnesty.org.uk/actions/end-inhumane-overuse-detention-now.

Apple, M. W. (1998). 'Foreword.' In J. L. Kincheloe, S. R. Steinberg, N. M. Rodriguez & R. E. Chennault (eds) *White Reign*. New York, NY: St Martin's Griffin.

Araujo, A. L. (2017). *Reparations for Slavery and the Slave Trade: A Transnational Comparative History*. London: Bloomsbury (kindle edition).

Ashe, S. D. & Nazroo, J. (2017). *Equality, Diversity and Racism in the Workplace: A qualitative analysis of the 2015 Race at Work Survey*. ESRC Centre on Dynamics of Ethnicity, University of Manchester.

Bateson, N. (2017). Liminal Leadership. *Kosmos: Journal for Global Transformation*. Retrieved from www.kosmosjournal.org/article/liminal-leadership, accessed on 26 September 2018.

Baum, B. (2008). *The Rise and Fall of the Caucasian Race: A Political History of Racial Identity*. New York, NY: New York University Press.

Bidol-Padva, P. (1972). *Developing New Perspectives on Race: An Innovative Multi-media Social Studies Curriculum in Racism Awareness for the Secondary Leve*. Detroit, MI: New Perspectives on Race.

Bloom, P. (2018). *Against Empathy: The Case for Rational Compassion*. London: The Bodley Head.

Bohm, D. (1996). *On Dialogue*. London, New York, NY: Routledge.

Bonnett, A. (2000). *White Identities: Historical and International Perspectives*. Harlow, London: Prentice Hall.

Brinkman, U. & Van Weedenburgh, O. (1999). The Intercultural Developmental Inventory: A New Tool for Improving Intercultural Rraining? Sietar Europe Conference: Trieste.

Buber, M. (2004). *I and Thou*. London and New York, NY: Continuum.

Cambell, J. & Oakes, J. (1998). 'The Invention of Race: Rereading White over Black.' In S. Delago, R. Stafancic & J. Stafancic (eds) *Critical White Studies*. Philadelphia, PA: Temple University Press.

Carey, T. A., Dudgeon, P., Hammond, S. W., Hirvonen, T., Kyios, M., Roufeil, L. & Smith, P. (2017). 'The Australian Psychological Society's apology to Aboriginal and Torres Strait islander people.' *Australian Psychologist*, 52(4), 261–267.

Carroll, M. & Shaw, E. (2013). *Ethical Maturity in the Helping Professions: Making Difficult Life and Work Decisions*. London: Jessica Kingsley Publishers.

Carter, H. (2003, 5 November). BBC racism exposé case dropped. *The Guardian*.

Cavanaugh, W. T. (2009). *The Myth of Religious Violence: Secular Ideology and the Roots of Modern Conflict*. Oxford: Oxford University Press.

Chatwin, B. (1987). *The Songlines*. London: Jonathan Cape.

Chomsky, N. (1999). *Profit over People: Neoliberalism and Global Order*. New York, NY: Seven Stories Press.

Coates, T.-N. (2017). *We Were Eight Years in Power*. London: Penguin Books.

Cockrane, L. (1994). *Adelard of Bath: The First English Scientist*. London: British Museum Press.

Corry, S. (2011). *Tribal Peoples for Tomorrow's World*. London: Freeman Press.

D'Ardenne, P. & Mantani, A. (1999). *Transcultual Counselling in Action*. London: Sage.

Dalal, F. (2002). *Race, Colour and Processes of Racialisation*. Hove, New York, NY: Brunner-Routledge.

de Graaf, J., Wann., D. & Naylor, T. H. (2014). *Affluenza: The All-Consuming Epidemic*. San Francisco, CA: Berrett-Koehler Publishers.

Dearden, N. (2016). Global Justice Now. Retrieved from https://www.globaljustice.org.uk//news/2016/sep/12/10-biggest-corporations-make-more-money-most-countries-world-combined accessed on 25 September 2018.

Deaton, A. (2013). *The Great Escape*. Princeton, NJ: Princeton University Press.

Deegan, H. (2011). *Politics South Africa* (2nd ed.). Abingdon and New York, NY: Routledge.

Delahanty, D. (2011). *The Psychobiology of Trauma and Resilience Across the Lifespan*. Lanham, MD: Jason Aronson.

Derrick, J. (2017). *Kahwà:tsire: Indigenous Families in a Family Therapy Practice with the Indigenous Worldview as the Foundation*. Retrieved from www.narcis.nl/publication/RecordID/oai%3Atilburguniversity.edu%3Apublications%2Fdd909f5b-253e-435d-9979-fbee39778032, accessed on 26 September 2018.

Derrick, J. (2018). The Box-Circle Experiential Exercice. Retrieved from www.4windswellness.ca/workshops-and-training/when-rabbit-met-turtle, accessed on 26 September 2018.

Diamond, J. (2013). *Guns, Germs and Steel*. London: Penguin Vintage.

Dominelli, L. (1988). *Anti Racist Social Work* (1st ed.). London: Macmillan.

Dominelli, L. (2006a). *Anti-Racist Social Work* (2nd ed.). Basingstoke: Macmillan.

Dominelli, L. (2006b). *Anti Oppressive Social Work Theory and Practice*. London: Macmillan.

Dyer, R. (1997). *White*. London: Routledge.

Eddo-Lodge, R. (2017). *Why I'm No Longer Talking to White People About Race*. London: Bloomsbury (kindle edition).

Elgot, J. (2018, 17 April). Theresa May's 'hostile environment' at heart of Windrush scandal. *The Guardian*.

Emejulu, A. (2016). 'On the Hideous Whiteness of Brexit.' In *The Brexit Crisis. A Verso Report*. London: Verso.

Emerson, R. W. (1975). *The Journals and Miscellaneuos Journals of Ralph Waldo Emerson* (W. Plumstead & W. H. Gilman (eds) Vol. X1 1848–1851). Cambridge, MA and London: Harvard University Press.

Emerson, R. W. (1977). *The Journals and Miscellaneous Notebooks of Ralph Waldo Emerson* (R. H. Orth & A. H. Ferguson (eds) Vol. X111 1852–1855). Cambridge, MA and London: Harvard University Press.

Fioramonti, L. (2016). *Wellbeing Economy*. Johannesburg: Pan Macmillan South Africa.

Francis, P. (2015, 2nd September). The Encyclical Letter of the Holy Father Francis. Laudato Si: On Care for Our Common Home. *Catholic Herald*. Retrieved from www.catholicherald. co.uk/news/2015/06/18/full-text-laudato-si, accessed on 26 September 2018.

Frankenberg, R. (1999). *Displacing Whiteness*. Durham and London: Duke University Press.

Frederickson, G. (1997). 'White Images of Black Slaves.' In R. Delgado & J. Stefancic (eds) *Critical White Studies: Looking Behind the Mirror*. Philadelphia, PA: Temple University.

Gapp, K. & Bohacek, J. (2017). 'Epigenetic germline inheritance in mammals: looking to the past to understand the future.' *Genes, Brain and Behavior*. doi:10.1111/gbb.12407.

Gov.UK. (2017). Hate Crime, England and Wales 2016 to 2017. Retrieved from www.gov.uk/government/statistics/hate-crime-england-and-wales-2016-to-2017, accessed on 26 September 2018.

Griffin, J. & Tirrell, I. (2005). *Freedom from Addiction: The Secret Behind Successful Addiction Busting (Human Givens Approach Series)* East Sussex: Human Givens Publishing Ltd.

The Guardian (2018, 7 February). First Modern Britons had 'Dark to Black' Skin, Cheddar Man DNA analysis reveal. Retrieved from www.theguardian.com/science/2018/feb/07/first-modern-britons-dark-black-skin-cheddar-man-dna-analysis-reveals, accessed on 26 September 2018.

Hanh, T. N. (2017). *The Art of Living: Peace and Freedom in the Here and Now*. San Francisco, CA: HarperOne (kindle edition).

Hannaford, I. (1996). *The History of an Idea in the West*. Washington, DC: The Woodrow Wilson Center Press.

Hansen, S. (2017). *Notes from a Foreign Country: An American Abroad in a Post-American World*. New York, NY: Farrar, Straus and Giroux.

Harari, Y. N. (2015). *Homo Deus*. London: Penguin Random House.

Hartman, E. (2016). *Wie Viele Sklaven Halten Sie*. Frankfurt, New York, NY: Campus Verlag.

Hawkins, P. (2017a). *Leadership Team Coaching in Practice*. Kogan Page.

Hawkins, P. (2017b). *Leadership Team Coaching* (3rd ed.). London: Kogan Page.

Hawkins, P. (2018). A Systemic Primer. Renewal Associates. Retrieved from www.renewalassociates.co.uk/wp-content/uploads/2016/08/A-Systemic-Primer-v4.pdf.

Hawkins, P. (2018, in press). 'Resourcing: The Neglected 3rd Leg of Supervision.' In S. Palmer &
E. Turne (eds) *The Heart of Supervision.*

Hawkins, P. & Shohet, R. (2012). *Supervision in the Helping Professions* (3rd ed.). Maidenhead:
Open University Press/Mcgraw Hill.

Hawkins, P. & Smith, N. (2006). *Coaching, Mentoring and Organizational Consultancy.* London:
McGraw Hill.

Hawkins, P. & Smith, N. (2013). 'Transformational Coaching.' In E. Cox, T. Bachirova & D.
Clutterbuck (eds) *The Complete Handbook of Coaching* (2nd ed.). London: Sage.

Heffernan, M. (2011). *Wilfull Blindness: Why We Ignore the Obvious.* London: Simon and
Schuster.

Hellinger, B. & Hovel, G. (1999). *Acknowledging What Is: Conversations with Bert Hellinger.*
Phoenix, AZ: Zeig, Tucker and Co.

Helms, J. E. (1995). *An Update of Helms' White and People of Colour Racial Identity Models.*
Handbook of Multicultural Counseling. Thousand Oaks, CA: Sage.

Henry, W. L. (2007). *Whiteness Made Simple.* London: Learning by Choice.

Herb, K. (2004). *Twelve-Step Guide to Using the Alcoholics Anonymous Big Book: Personal
Transformation: The Promise of the Twelve-Step Process.* Torrance, CA: Capizon Publishing.

Heuman, G. (2000). 'Riots and Resistance in the Caribbean at the Moment of Freedom.' In H.
Temperley (ed.) *After Slavery: Emancipation and its Discontents.* London and Portland, OR:
Frank Cass Publishers.

Hill Collins, P. & Bilge, S. (2016). *Intersectionality.* Malden, MA: Polity Press.

Hirsch, A. (2018). *Brit(ish): On Race, Identity and Belonging.* London: Penguin Vintage.

Hofstede, G. (1980). *Culture's Consequences: International Differences in Work-Related Values.*
London and Beverly Hills, CA: Sage.

Hübinette, T. & Lundström, C. (2011). 'Sweden after the recent election: the double-binding
power of Swedish Whiteness through the mourning of the loss of the "Old Sweden" and
the passing of the "Good Sweden".' *Nordic Journal of Feminist and Gender Research*, 10(1),
42–45.

Hübinette, T. & Lundström, C. (2015). 'Three phases of hegemonic whiteness: understanding
racial temporalities in Sweden.' *Social Identities: Journal for the Study of Race, Nation and
Culture*, 20:6. http://dx.doi.org/10.1080/13504630.2015.100482, accessed on 26 September
2018. doi:10.1080/13504630.2015.1004827, accessed on 26 September 2018.

Husain, S. (2012). *Are British Police Institutionally Racist? Memoirs of an Accused Conman.*
Bloomington, IN: AuthorHouse.

Hycner, R. & Jacobs, L. (1995). *The Healing Relationship in Gestalt Therapy: A Dialogic/Self
Psychology Approach.* New York, NY: The Gestalt Journal Press.

Irvin Painter, N. (2010). *The History of White People.* New York, NY and London: Norton
(kindle edition).

Irvin Painter, N. (2016). What Whiteness Means in the Trump Era. *The New York Times.*
Retrieved from www.nytimes.com/2016/11/13/opinion/what-whiteness-means-in-the-
trump-era.html, accessed on 26 September 2018.

Irving, D. (2014). *Waking Up White.* Winchester, MA: Elephant Room Press (kindle edition).

Jaccobson-Widding, A. (1979). *Red-White-Black as a Mode of Thought*. Uppsala: Acta Universitatis Upsaliensis.

Jacobs, L. (2005). 'For Whites Only.' In T. L. Bar-Joseph (ed.) *The Bridge: Dialogues Across Cultures* (pp. 225–244). Metairie/New Orleans, LA: Gestalt Institute Press.

Jacobs, L. (2016). 'Dialogue and double consciousness: lessons in power and humility.' *Gestalt Review*, 20(2), 147–161.

Jacobson, M. F. (1998). *Whiteness of a Different Color: European Immigrants and the Alchemy of Race*. Cambridge, MA and London: Harvard University Press.

Jacques, M. (2012). *When China Rules the World: The End of the Western World and the Birth of a New Global Order* (2nd ed.). London: Penguin Books.

Kegan, R. & Laskow Lahey, L. (2009). *Immunity to Change*. Boston, MA: Harvard University Press.

Kendi, I. X. (2016). *Stamped from the Beginning: The Definitive History of Racist Ideas in America*. London: The Bodley Head.

Khalili, L. (2016). *The Brexit Crisis. A Verso Report*. London: Verso.

Kincheloe, J. L. & Steinberg, S. R. (1998). 'Addressing the Crisis of Whiteness.' In J. L. Kincheloe, S. R. Steinberg, N. M. Rodriguez & R. E. Chennaut (eds) *White Reign*. New York, NY: St Martin's Griffin.

King, M. L. (1999). *The Autobiography of Martin Luther King Jr*. New York, NY: Warner Books.

Klebnikov, P. (2002). 'Theft of the century: privatization and the looting of Russia.' *The Multinational Monitor*, 23 (1 and 2), p.23.

Kline, R. (2014). The snowy white peaks of the NHS: a survey of discrimination in governance and leadership and the potential impact on patient care in London and England. Middlesex University's Research Repository.

Kluckhohn, F. L. & Strodtbeck, F. R. (1961). *Variations in Value Orientations*: Evanston, IL: Peterson and Company.

Kurlantzick, J. (2016). *State Capitalism: How the Return of Stalinism is Transforming the World*. Oxford: Oxford University Press.

Lago, C. (ed.) (2011). *The Handbook of Transcultural Counselling and Psychotherapy*. London: McGraw Hill.

Lanham, J. D. (2017). *Home Place: Memoirs of a Coloured Man's Love Affair with Nature*. Minneapolis, MN: Milkweed Editions.

Laungani, P. (2004). *Asian Perspectives in Counselling and Psychotherapy*. Hove: Brunner-Routledge.

Lennon, S. (2016). *The Failure of Multiculturalism*. New York, NY: Pine Hill Books.

Lilla, M. (2017). *The Once and Future Liberal: After Identity Politics*. New York, NY: Harper Collins.

Luce, E. (2017). *The Retreat of Western Liberalism*. London: Little, Brown Book Group (kindle edition).

Maçães, B. (2018). *The Dawn of Eurasia: On the Trail of the New World Order*. London: Penguin Books.

Macpherson, W. (1999). The Stephen Lawrence Inquiry. London: The Stationery Office.

Mahoney, M. R. (1997). 'Racial Construction and Women as Differentiated Actors.' In R. Delgado & J. Stefancic (eds) *Critical White Studies*. Philadelphia, PA: Temple University Press.

Manning, S. (2013, 3 March). The stately homes built on the back of slaves. *The Independent*.

Marx, K. (2013). *Capital* (M. Samuel & A. Aveling, Trans.). Ware, Hertfordshire: Wordsworth Editions Limited.

Maslow, A.H. (2014) *A Theory of Human Motivation*. Floyd, VA: Sublime Books.

May, G. (2013). *Bending Toward Justice: The Voting Rights Act and the Transformation of American Democracy* New York, NY: Basic Books (kindle edition).

McDonald Beckles, H. (2013). *Britain's Black Debt: Reparations for Caribbean Slavery and Native Genocide*. Kingston, Jamaica: University of the West Indies Press.

McIntosh, P. (1988). 'White Privilege and Male Privilege: A Personal Account of Coming to See Correspondences Through Work in Women's Studies.' *Race, Class and Gender: An Anthology*. Belmont, CA: Wadsworth.

Meadows, D., Randers, J. & Meadows, D. (2004). *Limits to Growth: The 30-Year Update*. White River Junction, VT: Chelsea Green Publishing Company.

Menzies, F. (2016). *A World of Difference*. Highett, Victoria: Major Street Publishing (kindle edition).

Michels, R. (1915). *Political Parties: A Sociological Study of the Oligarchical Tendencies of Modern Democracy* (E. P. Paul & C. Paul, Trans.). New York, NY: The Free Press.

Mills, C. (2005). Personal communication.

Moses, N. (2017). *Stolen, Smuggled, Sold: On the Hunt for Cultural Treasures*. Lanham, MD, Boulder, CO, London, New York, NY: Rowman and Littlefield.

Nicholoff, P. (1994). *Historical Introduction. The Collected Works of Ralph Waldo Emerson: English Traits*. Cambridge MA and London: The Harvard Press.

Nutt, D. & Nestor, L. (2013). *Addiction (Oxford Psychiatry Library)*. Oxford: Oxford University Press.

Olusoga, D. (2016). *Black and British: A Forgotten History*. London: Pan MacMillan.

Orange, D. (1997). *Emotional Understanding*. New York, NY, London: Guilford Press.

Patel, T. G. & Tyrer, D. (2011). *Race, Crime and Resistance*. London: Sage.

Piketty, T. (2014). *Capital in the 21st Century*. Cambridge, MA and London: The Belknap Press of Harvard University Press.

Pomerantsev, P. (2017). *Nothing is True and Everything is Possible: Adventures in Modern Russia*. London: Faber and Faber.

Powell, E. (1961). The Churchill Society. Retrieved from http://churchill-society-london.org.uk/StGeorge.html, accessed on 26 September 2018.

Quillian, L., Pager, D., Hexel, O. & Midtbøen, A. H. (2017). 'Meta-Analysis of Field Experiments Shows No Change in Racial Discrimination in Hiring over Time.' Retrieved from www.pnas.org/content/114/41/10870, accessed on 26 September 2018.

Rapatahana, V. & Bunce, P. (2012). 'Introduction: English Language as Thief.' In V. Rapatahana and P. Bunce (eds.) *English Language as Hydra: It's Impact on Non-English Language Cultures*. Bristol, Buffalo, Toronto: Multilingual Matters.

Reason, P. (1994). 'Towards a Participatory World View.' In P. Reason (ed.) *Participation in Human Inquiry*. London: Sage.

Reason, P. & Bradbury, H. (2001). 'Introduction: Inquiry and Participation in Search of a World Worthy of Human Aspiration.' In P. Reason & H. Bradley (eds) *Handbook of Action Research*. London: Sage.

Rieder, J. (2013). *Gospel of Freedom: Martin Luther King, Jr's Letter from Birmingham Jail and the Struggle that Changed a Nation*. New York, NY: Bloomsbury Press (kindle edition).

Ritchie, A. J. (2017). *Invisible No More: Police Violence Against Black Women and Women of Colour*. Boston, MA: Beacon Press (kindle edition).

Rosen, A. (2018a). Personal communication.

Rosen, A. (2018b). A Global Push for Mental Health Professionals to Apologise to Indigenous Peoples. Croakey: Independent. Retrieved from https://croakey.org.

Rosen, A. & Brideson, T. (2018). 'A Call for an International Apology from all Mental Health Professionals and Services to all Indigenous or First Peoples.' Transforming Australia's Mental Health Service Systems, Sydney, Australia.

Rotberg, R. I. (2009). *China into Africa*. Washington, DC: Brookings Institution Press.

Rudd, K. (2008). Apology to Australia's Indigenous Peoples. House of Representatives, Parliament House, Canberra. Retrieved from http://primeministers.naa.gov.au/primeministers/rudd/in-office.aspx#section6, accessed on 26 September 2018.

Ryde, J. (2005). Exploring White Racial Identity and its Impact on Psychotherapy and Psychotherapy Professions. PhD thesis, University of Bath.

Ryde, J. (2009). *Being White in the Helping Professions: Developing Effective Intercultural Awareness*. London: Jessica Kingsley Publishers.

Savage, M. (2015). *Social Class in the 21st Century*. London: Pelican.

Scharmer, O. (2009). *Theory U: Leading from the Future as it Emerges*. Oakland CA: Berrett-Koehler Publishers.

Shari'ati, A. (1980). *Marxism and Other Western Fallacies: An Islamic Critique*. Berkeley, CA: Mizan Press.

Sontag, S. (1967). 'What's happening to America?' *Partisan Review*, 34(1), 57–58.

Spiro, J. P. (2009). *Defending the Master Race: Conservation, Eugenics and the Legacy of Madison Grant*. Burlington, VT: University of Vermont Press.

Steger, M. B. & Roy, R. K. (2010). *Neoliberalism: A Very Short Introduction*. Oxford: Oxford University Press.

Stolorow, R. D. & Atwood, G. E. (1992). *Contexts of Being*. Hilldale, NJ: The Analytic Press.

StopWatch. (2018). www.stop-watch.org/your-area/area/metropolitan

Sue, D. W. & Sue, D. (1990). *Counselling the Culturally Different* (2nd ed.). New York, NY: Wiley.

Taplin, T. (2015). *Modern Day Slavery*. CreateSpace (kindle edition).

Taylor, A. J. P. (2001). *The Origins of the Second World War*. London: Penguin.

Thomas, A. (2017). *The Hate U Give*. New York, NY: Balzer and Bray.

Triandis, H. C. (1995). *Individualism and Collectivism*. Oxford and Boulder, CA: Westview Press.

Tutu, D. (1998). *Truth and Reconciliation Commission of South Africa Report*. Truth and Reconciliation Committees.

Tutu, D. & Tutu, M. A. (2014). *The Book of Forgiving*. London: HarperCollins.

Uloso, D. (2016). *Black and British: A Forgotten History*. London: Pan Books.

Vitale, A. & Ryde, J. (2016). 'Promoting male refugees' mental health after they have been granted leave to remain (refugee status).' *International Journal of Mental Health Promotion*, 18 (2) 106–125.

Walker, F. A. (1896). 'Restriction of immigration. *Atlantic Monthly* 77, June, 1896, 822–829. Retrieved from www.ucl.ac.uk/USHistory/Building/docs/Walker.htm, accessed on 26 September 2018.

Webb, S. L. (2017). *Colorsim: Essays and Poems*. Colour Healing (kindle edition).

Webber, C. (2018). A South Afrian Story of Wanting to be White, personal communication.

Wilkinson, R. & Pickett, K. (2009). *The Spirit Level*. London: Allen Lane (kindle edition).

Worthington, A. (2015). *The Guantanamo Files: The Stories of 774 Detainees in America's Illegal Prison*. London: Pluto Press.

Yontef, G. (1993). *Awareness, Dialogue and Process*. New York, NY: Gestalt Journal Press.

Subject Index

Author Index